Southern Living
easy
entertaining

Southern Living
easy
entertaining

Oxmoor
House

Southern Living® Easy Entertaining
©2002 by Oxmoor House, Inc.
Book Division of Southern Progress Corporation
P.O. Box 2463, Birmingham, AL 35201

Created especially for *Southern Living At HOME*™,
the Direct Selling Division of Southern Progress Corporation

For information about *Southern Living At HOME*™, please write to:
Consultant Services
P.O. Box 830951
Birmingham, AL 35282-8451

Library of Congress Control Number: 00-091846
ISBN: 0-8487-2560-3
Printed in the United States of America
Third Printing 2003

Many products featured in this book are from current
and previous *Southern Living At HOME*™ catalogs.
Current products are available for purchase.

Cover: *Satiny Mocha Torte (page 124)*
Back Cover: *Wedding Shower (page 44)*

Oxmoor House, Inc.
Editor-in-Chief: Nancy Fitzpatrick Wyatt
Executive Editor: Susan Carlisle Payne
Art Director: Cynthia R. Cooper
Copy Chief: Catherine Ritter Scholl

Southern Living At HOME™
Vice President and Executive Director: Dianne Mooney
Design Editor: Melanie Grant

Southern Living® Easy Entertaining
Editor: Susan Hernandez Ray
Designer: Clare T. Minges
Copy Editor: Jacqueline B. Giovanelli
Foods Editor: Julie Gunter
Editorial Assistant: McCharen Pratt
Test Kitchens Director: Elizabeth T. Luckett
Assistant Test Kitchens Director: Julie Christopher
Recipe Editor: Gayle Hays Sadler
Test Kitchens Staff: Kristi Carter, Jennifer A. Cofield,
Ana Price Kelly, Kathleen Royal Phillips, Jan A. Smith
Senior Photographer: Jim Bathie
Contributing Photographers: Ralph Anderson, Tina Cornett,
William Dickey, Brit Huckabay
Senior Photo Stylist: Kay E. Clarke
Contributing Photo Stylists: Buffy Hargett, Leslie Byars Simpson
Director, Production and Distribution: Phillip Lee
Associate Production Manager: Leslie Johnson
Production Assistant: Faye Porter Bonner
Contributing Proofreaders: Rebecca Behan, Dawn Russell

CONTENTS

KEEP IT SIMPLE

《 》

Creating the perfect atmosphere to welcome friends and family can be such a pleasure, but many times planning a party seems overwhelming. It's actually easier than you think. This book will share simple secrets that will give you more time to enjoy your get-togethers, while making your guests feel extra special.

PLAN AHEAD

Anything you can do before the party will help make things much easier on the day of the party. Our party countdown on page 10 helps you plan up to six weeks ahead of your event. Most of the recipes from our recipe chapters (appetizers, entrées, sides, and desserts) can be made ahead. The more you do to prepare for the party, the more you'll enjoy it. And nothing makes guests feel more at ease than a relaxed hostess.

CREATE 10-MINUTE CENTERPIECES

Wow your guests with arrangements that take just minutes to assemble. The secret is to have a few great containers on-hand. Whether you need something for the center of the table or the buffet, you'll find unique ideas beginning on page 20. Many of them don't even use fresh flowers, like the grouping of candy and candles (page 23) and the faux flowers (page 22).

FOLLOW AN EASY MENU PLAN

There are so many types of events that you can host—brunches, lunches, cocktail parties, and dinners, just to name a few. We've put together menu plans for a variety of occasions, beginning on page 26. All the recipes have an easy twist to them, as do the inviting table settings. For example, the recipes in our Champagne Dessert Party on page 46 are made from convenience products. And the centerpiece groups potted plants together in a beautiful tin bowl.

ENTERTAIN ANYWAY

You can still host a lovely party, even if you don't have a lot of time to spend in the kitchen. Each recipe chapter ends with easy, no-cook ideas for when you just don't have the time to spend in the kitchen; see pages 80, 98, 114, and 140. You can put together an entire party using inspiration from each of these four sections, or just pick and choose a few ideas. For example, if you'd like to have a Mexican Fiesta you can use the menu on page 30 or our No-Time-To-Cook idea on page 99. Add the chips and salsa suggestion from page 80, store-bought salad from page 114, and embellish a store-bought cake as on page 140 and 141. Party planning has never been so easy!

behind the
scenes

COUNTDOWN TO PARTY TIME

《 》

The secret to easy entertaining is planning ahead. Follow these guidelines to help get your party started.

FOUR TO SIX WEEKS AHEAD:

• Set the date and time.

• Make your guest list.

• Decide what you'll serve. Consult make-ahead recipe notes. On your calendar, write when you'll prepare or assemble each dish. Order any food you decide to have catered.

• Select invitations if you plan to send them for your party.

THREE WEEKS AHEAD:

• Mail holiday invitations. For informal events, send invitations two weeks in advance.

ONE TO TWO WEEKS AHEAD:

• Check your supply of chairs, serving dishes, flatware, and glassware.

• Make a grocery list. Shop for nonperishables.

• Give some thought to your home's exterior. Plant seasonal flowers in a planter on the front porch, hang a festive wreath, wash front-facing windows—anything to give your place a lift.

TWO TO THREE DAYS AHEAD:

• Get out china, serving dishes, and utensils. Polish silver.

• Shop for perishables.

• Clean house. If you're too busy, consider hiring a cleaning crew.

• Make place cards.

ONE DAY AHEAD:

• Plan a centerpiece. Buy flowers, or clip some from your garden.

• Prepare dishes that can be made ahead.

• Chill beverages. Make extra ice.

• Anticipate "guest geography." Arrange furniture to maximize seating, pulling service chairs from other rooms. Place occasional or folding tables nearby.

DAY OF THE EVENT:

• Set the table. Arrange the centerpiece.

• Finish preparing food, and arrange it on serving dishes. For a buffet or large party, fill additional trays so that you can replenish the table by exchanging a full tray for an empty one.

• Reserve some time for rest. If you're refreshed and relaxed, you'll be able to enjoy your party every bit as much as your guests will.

YOU'RE INVITED

«»

The party begins the moment that guests receive their invitations. Invitations give a quick preview of the party and the fun to be had. They also give guests all the necessary information—the date, time, place, type of party or occasion, names of the hosts, and the name and phone number or address to respond to, if requested.

USE YOUR CREATIVITY

The way invitations are presented generates excitement about a party. A bright, clever invitation is hard to resist; it makes the receiver think that the party can't be missed. Let loose the reigns of your imagination. Use a computer to create all sorts of lively invitations; either print on an existing invitation or design your own. For a small number of guests, you can even hand-deliver a special gift that gives all the necessary information. When a get-together is spontaneous, an invitation by phone or e-mail is appropriate.

PLEASE REPLY

Decide how you want guests to reply to your invitation. When "regrets only" appears on an invitation, it means guests respond only if they can't attend. Anytime R.S.V.P. appears, a reply of either acceptance or regret is required. If you need to calculate the quantity of food but guests still haven't responded, call and ask if they plan to attend. Even after you have received the responses, remember that there will probably be a few last-minute cancellations.

THE PLEASURE OF YOUR COMPANY

• Have a stationery budget in mind. If you have no idea what the cost might be, do a little homework before you place an order. If the cost blows your budget, you can save money by creating your own invitations.

• Be prepared when you visit the stationer. Know the date, time, and location.

• Double-check spelling.

• Order invitations well in advance so that you'll have time to address and mail them. Expect that it will take about a week for invitations to be printed.

SETTING UP THE BUFFET

‹‹ ››

A buffet is the most popular style of meal service, especially for large groups. Set the buffet on a dining table or other surface, such as a chest, kitchen counter, or sideboard, that will accommodate a stack of dinner plates and serving dishes of food. Since your guests will serve themselves, arrange the buffet using these tips:

• Place serving dishes in an arrangement that allows for easy circulation and traffic flow.

• Set the buffet near the kitchen so that it's easy to refill serving dishes.

• If a dish is to be served over rice, locate the rice first in line.

• Place dressings and sauces close to the dish they complement.

• Serve desserts at one end of the buffet, or place them on a serving cart.

• Arrange beverages on a side table, or serve them from a tray after guests are seated.

SETTING THE TABLE

‹‹ ››

Tablesettings give you a chance to be creative in coordinating colors, dishes, glasses, and flatware. When planning your arrangement keep in mind the order in which dishes, glasses, and flatware will be used. Set the table using the tips below as a guide so that guests will easily know which item to use when.

• Lay place mats flush with the table edge or about 1 inch from the edge.

• Fold the napkins, and lay them on the place mat to the left of the forks.

• Aim to keep the amount of flatware that will be used to a minimum. Generally, there should be no more than three pieces of flatware on each side of the plate.

• Put knives and spoons to the right of the plate, with each knife's cutting edge facing the plate. Forks go to the left of the plate.

• As a general rule, "start from the outside and work your way in." That is, the flatware for the first course is on the outside, farthest from the plate.

• Place water glasses above the knife. Position additional glasses in order of use.

• Place bread-and-butter plates near the tip of the fork. If there is no bread-and-butter plate, place the salad plate there instead.

• If there is a bread-and-butter plate, place the salad plate to the left and a little below the bread-and-butter plate.

EASY ETIQUETTE

<< ‹ › >>

Here are a few things to keep in mind

when you're hosting an event:

• For formal service, present a served dinner plate from the left of each guest; remove plates from the right.

• For family-style service, pass bowls and platters of food around the table to the right.

• Serve and remove beverages from the right with the right hand. Be careful not to collide with other beverage glasses.

• Pick up a guest's glass at the stem or the base, never near or over the top.

• Refill coffee cups and glasses without removing them from the table.

• Keep a napkin in your left hand to wipe drips from coffee pots or water pitchers.

• As the hostess, take your first bite as soon as you're seated. Guests will take their cue to begin eating from you. Once you pick up a piece of flatware, never place it back on the table; rest it on your plate. Leave the knife at the upper plate edge with its blade toward the plate. Leave the fork centered on the plate.

• Remove salt, pepper, butter, and excess flatware from the table after the main course is cleared away.

PARTY POINTERS

《 》

WHEN TO ENTERTAIN

Reasons to get together with family and friends are endless—birthdays and holidays are obvious opportunities to throw a party, but there's no need to wait for an occasion. Invent your own—a relaxed weekend brunch with neighbors, lunch before a football game, or a casual dinner before an evening at the movies. And entertaining doesn't have to be centered around a complete meal. Other possibilities include coffees, afternoon teas, cocktail parties, dessert parties—the list goes on.

CHOOSING THE LOCATION

Almost any place that suggests a particular mood can be a party site. Create a welcoming setting on a table in a pretty garden (see page 44). Or stir up your desire for adventure by packing a party in laundry hampers and serving up a game-day tailgate brunch (see page 28).

Invariably, some of the best places to entertain are right at home. Try placing a table in front of the fireplace. Or clear off a corner of the front porch, and dress up a table with festive linens. Stretch your creativity by decorating your basement with southwestern flair for a Tex-Mex fiesta (see page 30).

FORMAL VS. INFORMAL

Most formal events are still seated affairs, with the hostess being particularly mindful of etiquette (see opposite page). But busy lifestyles have led to the desire for more casual entertaining. Informal get-togethers open the door to stand-up cocktail parties, breakfasts, serve-yourself buffets, casual brunches, small lunches, and impromptu dinners.

ALL THROUGH
THE HOUSE

《 》

Beautiful arrangements

aren't just for the center of

the table. These ideas can be used

to decorate your entire house.

PITCHER THIS
A pitcher of flowers flanked by tapers tied
with greenery adds a nice touch to an empty
table—or even the kitchen counter.

BOWL OF BEAUTY
A bowl full of fruit with a hint of flowers
and greenery looks great on a sideboard or a
chest. Candlesticks ringed with flowers and
fruit add height to the grouping.

18

DAISY DRESS-UP

A charming little vase of gerbera daisies can pop up just about any- >> where—from a coffee table, to a side table, to a counter in the bathroom.

ALL AGLOW

<< The soft glow of candlelight adds to the atmosphere of a party. Glass candlesticks topped with small daisy rings placed around the house create a festive mood.

10-MINUTE CENTERPIECES FOR TABLES

《 ‹ 》

Wow your guests with great-looking arrangements that take very little time to assemble. Keep centerpieces at a height that allows for good eye contact among guests.

⌃⌃

SUNNY AND ROSY

Combine sunflowers and roses for a colorful mix. First, soak some florist's foam, and place it in a container. Then arrange the roses in your hands, and cut the stems to the right length. Stick the stems into the foam. Fill in with sunflowers, being sure to cover the foam.

CANDLE CLIQUE

This grouping of candles makes a quaint display in the center of a small table. A decorative tile serves as a base and ties the candles together. A few flowers placed on the side add a soft touch.

HANGING OF GREENERY

Centerpieces don't necessarily need to be on the table. Guests can easily converse beneath this chandelier adorned with candy canes and greenery.

»

«

FALL FOR COPPER

A shallow copper bowl makes an ideal container for a combination of colorful pumpkins and gourds. Leaves and berries add texture. Fruit, such as apples, pears, and oranges, could be substituted for the pumpkins.

10-MINUTE CENTERPIECES FOR BUFFETS

‹‹ ››

*Tall arrangements command attention
on buffets and work better there than
on the dining table.*

METAL PETALS

Faux flowers take on a whole new meaning with these
metal blooms. The biggest benefit is that you can use
them again and again. Fresh hydrangeas at the top of
the container provide a soft contrast.

GRAND STAND

A cake stand adds height to this easy-to-build arrangement. Simply soak a block of florist's foam, and place it
on the center of the stand. Add oranges to the base.
Place roses in the foam above the oranges, and top with
tapers. Use greenery, berries, and nuts to fill in any holes.

BUNDLES OF BLOOMS

An arrangement of urns can be as simple or intricate as the hostess wishes, depending on the number of urns and materials used. Roses, fruits, and vegetables are at the heart of this elegant display. Coordinate the fruits and vegetables used to match the food served.

»

HOW SWEET IT IS

These bell jar urns filled with candy and candles are unique alternatives to flowers. Tall pillar candles or a grouping of tapers could also substitute for the pillars pictured.

«

SIMPLE TOUCHES

«»

*These easy ideas will help make
your party guests feel pampered.*

⌃

PACK A PARTY

Textured sacks and boxes make convenient
containers for serving a meal. They're
especially handy for guests on the
go—such as those headed to a ball game
or an outdoor event.

«

FLOWER POWER

Elevate plain linens by tying them with
ribbon and tucking in a flower.

SNAPPY IDEA

Place cards add a touch of elegance to the table. In this case, a place card attached to a string of sugar snap peas and wrapped around a candle is just right for a few guests. For more guests, consider writing names on decorative paper and tying the cards to napkins with sugar snap peas and raffia.

》》

BLOOMING BUCKET

《《

A bucket of fresh flowers at the front gate makes a cheery welcome. This arrangement also looks stunning on a door or a window in a room where guests will gather.

our menu
parade

TAILGATE PARTY

<< *serves 8* >>

Blue Cheese Rolls *(page 55)*
Crackers

Fried Chicken Fingers with
Come-Back Sauce *(page 63)*

Black Bean Wraps *(page 97)*

Sweet 'n' Hot Green Beans
and Carrots *(page 106)*

Minted Iced Tea *(page 76)*
Assorted beers

Gather the gang, invite your neighbors, or surprise your family with this festive fall spread. Make-ahead fare and creative entertaining ideas guarantee this menu will score with your fans. Play classic Fried Chicken Fingers with Come-Back Sauce against sporty favorites—sassy Sweet 'n' Hot Green Beans and Carrots, Black Bean Wraps, and Blue Cheese Rolls. This game-day spread is a winner!

MEXICAN FIESTA

« *serves 6 to 8* »

Creamy Guacamole *(page 50)*

Colorful Salsa *(page 51)*
Tortilla chips

Mexican Pizza *(page 65)*

Taco-Chicken Skewers *(page 64)*

Margaritas and Mock Margaritas *(page 78)*

The bright colors and unique flavors of these recipes suggest a lively time is at hand. Pots of colorful flowers provide an easy and festive tablescape. Nibble on Taco-Chicken Skewers and enjoy spicy Mexican Pizza with salsa and chips for a light fiesta lunch or dinner. Our recipes include timesaving make-ahead tips.

GARDEN PARTY

<< *serves 12* >>

Tomato-Basil Dip *(page 52)*
Fresh veggies

Rosemary Pork Tenderloin
Roasted Red Pepper Sauce *(page 88)*
Cocktail rolls

Gourmet chips

Chewy Almond-Fudge Bars *(page 118)*

Minted Iced Tea *(double recipe, page 76)*
Bottled drinks

*I**f you enjoy entertaining outdoors,
our garden bench buffet is the perfect way to end
a summer day. Try these ideas to create an atmosphere that celebrates this casual time of year:*

• *Put your potting bench to full use as the
serving center (see far right photo).*
• *Place a freshly cut bundle of zinnias in a
hollowed-out melon (see left, middle photo).*
• *Use your wheelbarrow for ice and bottled
drinks (see left, bottom photo).*

SPRINGTIME BRUNCH

《 *serves 12 to 15* 》

Tomato-Basil Dip *(page 52)*
Steamed asparagus

Double-Stuffed Eggs *(page 60)*

"Eggstra" Special Chicken Salad *(page 57)*
Crackers

Baked Ham with Bourbon Glaze *(page 84)*
Biscuits   Beehive Butter *(pages 53)*

Fresh Fruit with
Celery-Poppy Seed Dressing *(page 103)*

Sunny Spring Lemonade
(double recipe, page 77)

elebrate the glorious gift of spring with a colorful brunch, most of which can be prepared ahead. This menu brings together an artful collection of traditional dishes with ingenious twists. The centerpiece is simple to create with an abundance of flower, herb, and vegetable transplants. Arranged to look like a spring garden, the collection can later be transferred to containers and flowerbeds. Assemble the table garden ahead so that the day of your gathering is relaxed and easy.

TIME FOR A TEA PARTY

《 *serves 6* 》

Savory Petits Fours *(page 71)*
with choice of fillings

Shortbread Cookie Hearts *(page 123)*

Minted Iced Tea *(page 76)*

A tray of artistically decorated miniature sandwiches can transform a simple gathering into a special occasion. Dainty shortbread cookies provide a sweet finale. To get a head start on your celebration, stir together several of our savory spreads, and store them in the refrigerator. Then follow these tips for creating picture-perfect party sandwiches.

- *Freeze the bread before filling.*
- *Assemble and slice the sandwiches while the bread is still partially frozen.*
- *Cover the sandwiches with damp paper towels until all are assembled; then wrap them individually with plastic wrap, and store them in the refrigerator up to 1 day before serving.*
- *Garnish the sandwiches, and arrange them on trays just before serving.*

ONE-DISH DELISH'

<< *serves 7 or 8* >>

Choice of Casserole:
Saucy Manicotti *(page 92)*
Chicken Enchilada Casserole *(page 90)*
Rich Seafood Casserole *(page 94)*

Mixed green salad with choice of
Italian, Ranch, or Caesar dressing

Bakery rolls

Choice of dessert from
The Grande Finale chapter *(pages 116–141)*

Dinner's a cinch when you take
your pick from these three one-dish meal
options—just add a simple salad, crusty
bakery bread, and choice of dessert from The
Grande Finale chapter. All the casseroles can
be made ahead and frozen. To make the table
decoration, simply place florist's foam in the center
of a decorative pot. Add sunflowers in the
center, and cover the base with parsley, rosemary,
cherry tomatoes, and green beans.

APPETIZERS APLENTY

*D*azzle your guests with an
impressive buffet of hearty appetizers.
What's the secret behind this sensational spread?
All the recipes are make-ahead.
Pick three or all eight of these treats.
As a general rule, when appetizers
precede a meal, three selections are plenty.
*When appetizers **are** the meal,*
plan on six to eight offerings.

DINNER FOR ANY OCCASION

<< *serves 8* >>

Spinach Salad with
Hot Citrus Dressing *(page 105)*

Rosemary Pork Tenderloin
Roasted Red Pepper Sauce *(page 88)*

Twice-Baked Potato Casserole *(page 112)*

Green Bean Bundles *(page 107)*

Bakery rolls

Choice of dessert from
The Grande Finale chapter *(pages 116–141)*

Whenever there's reason to celebrate—an anniversary, a birthday, or a promotion—this mostly make-ahead dinner can be ready on the double. For a simple and festive centerpiece, fill a container with pots of gerbera daisies and place oranges around the pots. For a fragrant touch, tuck rosemary sprigs into the napkin rings.

WEDDING SHOWER

<< *serves 12* >>

Sherried Chicken-and-Grape Salad,
(*double recipe, page 96*)

Parmesan Cheese Bites (*page 58*)

Sliced melon

Shortbread Cookie Hearts (*page 123*)
or bakery petits fours

Sunny Spring Lemonade (*page 77*)

Welcome guests to celebrate upcoming nuptials—or any special event—over a delectable menu for twelve. Entertain with ease using our make-ahead menu. The cookies and cheese bites can be baked days ahead, while the chicken salad can be prepared up to a day early. You can buy cut melon from the produce section of your grocery store. And, if you don't have time to make dessert, purchase a dozen petits fours from the bakery.

Chewy Almond-
Fudge Bars

White Chocolate
Charlotte Russe

CHAMPAGNE DESSERT PARTY

《 *serves 12* 》

Satiny Mocha Torte *(page 124)*

Chewy Almond-Fudge Bars *(page 118)*

Brandied Eggnog Trifle *(page 139)*

Irish Cream Tortoni Cups *(page 131)*

White Chocolate Charlotte Russe *(page 132)*

Champagne   Coffee

*W*hat could be sweeter than a party celebrating dessert? Convenience products do all the work in these desserts that contain eight ingredients or less. They're perfect for Christmas, but all except the Brandied Eggnog Trifle work well year-round. Pick three of the recipes to serve 10 to 12 guests, or offer all five to satisfy up to 20 guests. Tortoni served over ice, champagne chilled in a tin planter, and pots of flowers in a tin bowl add special touches.

party
starters

CREAMY GUACAMOLE

*Picante sauce punches up the flavor of this easy guacamole
that has no chopping or dicing. Pictured on page 31.*

4 ripe avocados, peeled and seeded
1 (8-ounce) package light cream cheese,
   softened
½ cup picante sauce
2 tablespoons lemon juice
1 teaspoon garlic salt
Garnish: chopped tomato

Mash avocados and cream cheese with a fork or potato masher. Stir in picante sauce, lemon juice, and garlic salt. Cover and chill up to 2 hours, if desired. Garnish, if desired. Serve with tortilla chips. Yield: 3 cups.

COLORFUL SALSA

Garden-fresh tomatoes brighten this chunky salsa. Pictured on page 31.

3 large tomatoes, chopped
2 (4.5-ounce) cans chopped green chiles
1 small onion, finely chopped
¼ cup chopped ripe olives
⅓ cup chopped fresh cilantro
3 tablespoons fresh lime juice
2 garlic cloves, pressed
½ teaspoon salt
½ teaspoon pepper
1 jalapeño pepper, seeded and chopped
    (optional)

Stir together first 9 ingredients and, if desired, jalapeño pepper; cover and chill at least 1 hour. Serve with tortilla chips. Yield: 3 cups.

TOMATO-BASIL DIP

Make the dip up to 2 days ahead, and chill until ready to serve with
crisp, fresh asparagus, carrots, celery, or radishes. Pictured on page 34.

1 cup mayonnaise
½ cup sour cream
½ cup chopped fresh basil
1 tablespoon tomato paste
1 tablespoon grated lemon rind
Garnish: fresh basil leaves

Whisk together first 5 ingredients until blended. Chill up to 2 days, if desired. Garnish, if desired. Yield: 1¾ cups.

BEEHIVE BUTTER

*This spicy butter tastes great slathered on ham biscuits. Bake our ham (recipe on page 84),
or purchase a sliced baked ham. Pictured on page 34.*

1 ½ cups butter, softened
½ cup spicy brown mustard
1 cup finely chopped pecans, toasted
1 pecan half
Garnishes: fresh herbs, edible flower petals

Stir together first 3 ingredients.

Form butter mixture into a beehive shape. Smooth mound with a spatula or rounded knife. Form grooves around mound with tines of a fork. Insert pecan half near the base for a door; chill 2 hours or up to 2 days. Garnish, if desired. Yield: 3 cups.

BRIE IN BRAIDED BREAD RING

A package of frozen bread dough is the secret behind the presentation of this appetizer. Pictured on page 41.

⅓ cup sliced almonds
⅓ cup sesame seeds*
1 (35.2-ounce) Brie round
3 tablespoons apricot or pineapple
    preserves
½ cup dried cranberries
½ cup diced candied pineapple
Braided Bread Ring
French baguette slices, toasted

Bake almonds and sesame seeds separately in 2 shallow pans at 350°, stirring occasionally, 5 to 10 minutes or until toasted. (Do not burn.)

Trim rind from top of Brie; brush preserves over top. Arrange almonds, sesame seeds, cranberries, and pineapple over preserves. Place Brie in center of Braided Bread Ring; serve with toasted French baguette slices. Yield: 20 servings.

*Poppy seeds may be substituted for sesame seeds; do not toast.

BRAIDED BREAD RING:

½ (32-ounce) package frozen bread dough, thawed

Place 2 large rimless baking sheets close together on oven rack, creating one large baking sheet at least 15 inches; grease.

Divide dough into thirds; roll each portion into a 36-inch rope, and braid. Grease outside of a 9-inch round cakepan, and place in center of prepared baking sheets. Wrap braid around cakepan, pinching ends together to seal.

Cover braid, and let rise in a warm place (85°), free from drafts, 1 hour or until doubled in bulk.

Bake at 375° for 18 to 20 minutes or until golden brown. Remove from oven; cool on a wire rack. Yield: 1 (15-inch) ring.

BLUE CHEESE ROLLS

Prepare these ahead and freeze, if you'd like. Just thaw them
in the refrigerator overnight. Pictured on page 29.

2 (8-ounce) packages cream cheese,
     softened
1 (8-ounce) package sharp Cheddar cheese
     slices, cut up
2 (4-ounce) packages crumbled blue cheese
½ small onion, diced
1½ tablespoons Worcestershire sauce
½ teaspoon ground red pepper
1½ cups finely chopped toasted pecans,
     divided
1½ cups finely chopped fresh parsley,
     divided

Process first 6 ingredients in a food processor 1 to 2 minutes, stopping to scrape down sides.

Stir together cheese mixture, 1 cup pecans, and ½ cup parsley. Cover and chill 1 hour.

Shape cheese mixture into 4 (7-inch) logs. Combine remaining ½ cup pecans and 1 cup parsley. Roll logs in parsley mixture; cover and chill. Serve with crackers. Yield: 4 (7-inch) logs.

MANGO CHUTNEY TORTA

The garnishes topping this loaf-shaped torta hint at the flavors inside.

1 cup low-fat cottage cheese
2 (8-ounce) packages cream cheese,
    softened
1 teaspoon curry powder
1 (9-ounce) jar mango chutney, divided
1 cup dry-roasted peanuts, divided
1 cup sliced green onions, divided
1 cup golden raisins, divided
Garnishes: sliced green onions, chopped
    peanuts, toasted flaked coconut

Process cottage cheese in a food processor until smooth. Add cream cheese and curry powder; process until smooth. Reserve half of cheese mixture.

Add 2 tablespoons chutney and half each of peanuts, green onions, and raisins to remaining cheese mixture; pulse 3 or 4 times or until coarsely chopped. Spoon into an 8- x 4-inch loafpan lined with plastic wrap; spread with ¼ cup chutney.

Pulse reserved cheese mixture, 2 tablespoons chutney, and remaining half each of peanuts, green onions, and raisins in processor 3 or 4 times or until coarsely chopped; spoon over torta. Cover and chill 8 hours.

Invert onto a serving plate. Top with remaining chutney, if desired. Garnish, if desired. Serve with crackers. Yield: 15 appetizer servings.

"EGGSTRA" SPECIAL CHICKEN SALAD

The egg's "stripes" are formed with green onion stems. Quickly dip the stems in boiling water to make them pliable. Pictured on page 34.

4 cups finely chopped cooked chicken
3 (8-ounce) packages cream cheese, softened*
¾ cup golden raisins, chopped
½ cup flaked coconut, toasted
2 celery ribs, diced
6 green onions, minced
⅓ cup chopped slivered almonds, toasted
1 tablespoon curry powder
½ teaspoon salt
½ teaspoon pepper
1 tablespoon freshly grated ginger
Garnishes: green onion stems, minced green onions, toasted flaked coconut, pistachios, fresh dill sprigs, yellow squash wedges, fresh chives, mixed salad greens, pansies, cucumber slices

Stir together all ingredients except garnishes. Form into an egg shape on a serving plate. Cover and chill 8 hours. Garnish, if desired. Serve with crackers. Yield: 20 to 25 appetizer servings.

* Reduced-fat cream cheese may be substituted for regular cream cheese.

PARMESAN CHEESE BITES

For easy slicing, use dental floss to cut the dough for these thick crackers. Place it under the dough, and criss-cross the ends over the top to slice through the dough. Pictured on pages 44 and 45.

1 cup all-purpose flour
⅔ cup grated Parmesan cheese
¼ teaspoon ground red pepper
½ cup butter or margarine, cut up
2 tablespoons milk

Pulse first 4 ingredients in a food processor until blended.

Shape dough into 2 (4-inch) logs. Wrap in plastic wrap, and place in an airtight container. Chill 8 hours. (Freeze up to 3 weeks, if desired; thaw in refrigerator overnight.)

Cut dough into ¼-inch-thick slices, and place on a lightly greased baking sheet. Brush with milk.

Bake at 350° for 12 to 15 minutes or until lightly browned. Yield: about 2½ dozen.

CHEDDAR DATES

Even if you don't like dates, you'll find these hard to resist.
Toasted pecans hide inside dates baked in balls of Cheddar pastry.

1 ½ cups (6 ounces) shredded sharp
    Cheddar cheese
1 cup all-purpose flour
2 tablespoons chopped fresh rosemary
1 teaspoon salt
⅓ cup butter or margarine, melted
24 pitted dates
24 pecan halves, toasted
1 egg white, lightly beaten
¼ teaspoon sugar

Combine first 4 ingredients in a bowl, stirring well. Add butter, stirring just until dry ingredients are moistened. (Dough will be crumbly.)

Make a lengthwise slit in each date, and stuff each with a pecan half. Press 1 generous tablespoon cheese mixture around each date, covering completely. Cover and chill 45 minutes. (You can cover and freeze dates up to 1 month.)

Place dates on a greased baking sheet, and brush with egg white. Sprinkle with sugar. Bake at 350° for 25 minutes. Remove dates to a wire rack to cool. Serve warm or at room temperature. Yield: 2 dozen.

DOUBLE-STUFFED EGGS

One basic recipe makes two variations to chill overnight.

1 dozen hard-cooked eggs, peeled
¾ cup light mayonnaise
½ cup instant potato flakes
1 tablespoon Dijon mustard
¼ teaspoon salt
¼ teaspoon pepper
Garnish: fresh dill sprigs

Cut eggs in half lengthwise. Remove yolks. Process yolks, mayonnaise, and next 4 ingredients in a food processor until smooth, stopping to scrape down sides.

Spoon filling into egg whites. Cover and chill up to 8 hours. Garnish, if desired. Yield: 2 dozen.

Bacon-Stuffed Eggs: Stir ⅔ cup (8 slices) cooked crumbled bacon, 3 tablespoons pickle relish, and ¼ cup chopped fresh chives into egg mixture. Proceed as directed.

Shrimp-Stuffed Eggs: Stir ¾ pound chopped cooked shrimp, 2 tablespoons prepared horseradish, and 6 minced green onions into egg mixture. Proceed as directed.

ROASTED PEPPER STRIPS ON ENDIVE

To save time, use strips of jarred roasted red peppers instead of roasting them yourself. Pictured on page 40.

1 large red bell pepper
¼ cup olive oil
1½ tablespoons balsamic vinegar
1½ tablespoons minced fresh parsley
¼ teaspoon salt
1 garlic clove, minced
Pinch of white pepper
6 heads Belgian endive
Garnish: fresh parsley sprigs

Bake bell pepper on an aluminum foil-lined baking sheet at 500° for 20 minutes or until pepper looks blistered; turn once.

Place pepper in a heavy-duty zip-top plastic bag; seal and let stand 10 minutes to loosen skin. Peel pepper; remove and discard seeds. Cut pepper into 2- x ¼-inch strips.

Stir together olive oil and next 5 ingredients; add pepper strips. Cover and chill 8 hours.

Slice stem end from endive, and separate leaves. Place a pepper strip on each endive leaf. Cover leaves with a damp towel, and refrigerate until ready to serve. Garnish with parsley sprigs, if desired. Yield: about 30 appetizers.

CHICKEN-AND-ARTICHOKE TARTS

If you want to make the tart shells ahead, store them in an airtight container up to 1 week. You can make the chicken mixture ahead, as well. Cover and chill up to 1 day.

1 (15-ounce) package refrigerated
   piecrusts
2 cups diced cooked chicken
⅔ cup coarsely chopped pecans, toasted
1 (14-ounce) can artichoke hearts, drained
   and chopped
3 tablespoons mayonnaise
3 tablespoons sour cream
3 green onions, minced
1 garlic clove, minced
½ teaspoon salt
½ teaspoon ground black pepper
¼ teaspoon ground red pepper

Unfold 1 piecrust, and press out fold lines; cut with a 2½-inch round cutter. Repeat procedure with remaining piecrust, rerolling and cutting dough scraps. Press rounds into 1-inch tart pans, trimming edges as needed, and place on baking sheets. Cover and freeze 15 minutes.

Bake tart shells on baking sheets at 425° for 5 to 6 minutes or until golden brown. Cool in pans on wire racks 10 minutes. Remove from pans, and cool on wire racks.

Stir together chicken and remaining 9 ingredients; spoon evenly into tart shells. Serve immediately, or chill up to 6 hours. Yield: about 5 dozen.

FRIED CHICKEN FINGERS WITH COME-BACK SAUCE

Save time by serving purchased chicken fingers with this sauce that's true to its name. Pictured on page 28.

8 skinned and boned chicken breast halves
2 cups milk
1 teaspoon salt
½ teaspoon lemon pepper
½ teaspoon black pepper
2 cups all-purpose flour
Vegetable oil
Garnish: gourmet salad greens
Come-Back Sauce

Cut each breast half into 4 strips.

Combine strips, milk, and next 3 ingredients in a shallow dish or heavy-duty zip-top plastic bag. Cover or seal, and chill 4 hours.

Remove chicken, discarding marinade; dredge in flour.

Pour oil to a depth of 2 inches into a large Dutch oven; heat to 350°. Fry chicken, in batches, 5 to 6 minutes or until golden. Drain on paper towels. Garnish, if desired. Serve with Come-Back Sauce. Yield: 16 appetizer servings or 8 main-dish servings.

COME-BACK SAUCE:

1 cup mayonnaise
½ cup olive oil
⅓ cup chili sauce
¼ cup ketchup
2 tablespoons water
4 teaspoons Worcestershire sauce
4 teaspoons prepared mustard
2 teaspoons coarsely ground pepper
⅛ teaspoon paprika
¼ teaspoon hot sauce
1 medium onion, minced
2 garlic cloves, minced

Stir together all ingredients. Cover and chill at least 1 hour, or up to 2 days ahead. Yield: 3 cups.

TACO-CHICKEN SKEWERS

Taco seasoning spices up the skewers and the dipping sauce for this easy appetizer. Pictured on page 31.

1 (8-ounce) container sour cream
1 (7-ounce) jar green salsa
2 tablespoons chopped fresh cilantro
1 (1.25-ounce) envelope taco seasoning
    mix, divided
4 skinned and boned chicken breast halves,
    cut into 1-inch pieces
Garnish: fresh cilantro leaves

Combine first 3 ingredients and 1 teaspoon taco seasoning mix in a bowl, stirring well. Cover and chill up to 8 hours, if desired.

Toss chicken with remaining taco seasoning mix. Cook chicken in a large nonstick skillet coated with vegetable cooking spray over medium-high heat 6 to 8 minutes or until done. Serve immediately, or cover and chill up to 2 hours. Serve on skewers with salsa mixture. Garnish, if desired. Yield: 8 appetizer servings.

MEXICAN PIZZA

This appetizer also works well as a main dish—just add a salad. Pictured on page 31.

1 (15-ounce) can kidney beans, rinsed and
    drained
2 teaspoons vegetable oil
¼ teaspoon ground cumin
¼ teaspoon chili powder
1 garlic clove, pressed
1 (4.5-ounce) can chopped green chiles
8 (8-inch) flour tortillas
½ cup salsa
1 small onion, diced
½ green bell pepper, diced
3 tablespoons sliced ripe olives
1 cup (4 ounces) shredded mozzarella
    cheese

Mash beans with a fork; stir in oil and next 4 ingredients.

Place 4 tortillas on greased baking sheets; spread with bean mixture. Top each with 1 tablespoon salsa; sprinkle with onion and bell pepper. Top with remaining tortillas, spreading each with 1 tablespoon salsa; sprinkle with olives and cheese.

Bake at 400° for 12 to 15 minutes. Yield: 8 appetizer servings or 4 main-dish servings.

OYSTER-SAUSAGE BUNDLES

Make-ahead appetizers couldn't be easier than these hearty bundles. Prepare them up to a week in advance and freeze them; bake them without thawing, when ready to serve.

½ pound Italian sausage
⅓ cup minced onion
1 (10-ounce) container fresh oysters
½ cup (2 ounces) shredded mozzarella
    cheese
¼ cup (1 ounce) shredded sharp Cheddar
    cheese
1 (17.25-ounce) package frozen puff
    pastry sheets, thawed

Remove and discard casings from sausage. Cook sausage and onion in a large skillet, stirring until sausage crumbles and is no longer pink. Drain well, and return to skillet.

Stir oysters gently into sausage mixture; cook over medium heat 1 to 2 minutes or just until edges of oysters curl. Remove from heat, and drain well; cool. Stir in cheeses.

Unfold pastry sheets onto a lightly floured surface. Cut each sheet into 8 rectangles; roll each rectangle into a 5-inch square.

Place sausage mixture evenly in middle of each pastry square. Pull up sides of pastry to enclose sausage mixture; twist ends, pinching to seal at neck and spreading open top edges of pastry. Place in an airtight container, and freeze 1 hour or up to 1 week.

Place bundles on an ungreased baking sheet. Bake at 400° for 20 to 22 minutes or until golden; serve immediately. Yield: 16 appetizers.

MARINATED STUFFED SHRIMP

All the initial assembly can be done 24 hours in advance. Save the last quick dip of the shrimp in the marinade for just before guests arrive, and then arrange the shrimp on serving plates.

1 pound unpeeled, large fresh shrimp
2 garlic cloves, minced
1 teaspoon salt
1 teaspoon freshly ground black pepper
2 tablespoons olive oil
1 (8-ounce) round smoked Gouda cheese
4 ounces prosciutto or country ham, thinly sliced
½ cup olive oil
¼ cup white balsamic vinegar
2 tablespoons chopped fresh rosemary
⅛ teaspoon ground red pepper

Peel shrimp, and devein, if desired. Make a deep slit down back of each shrimp, cutting to, but not through, inside curve of shrimp.

Sauté shrimp and next 3 ingredients in 2 tablespoons hot oil in a skillet 3 minutes or until shrimp turn pink; cool. (To make ahead, cover and chill until ready to assemble, up to 24 hours.)

Cut cheese into 24 (1-inch) cubes. Cut prosciutto into 24 thin strips. (To make

ahead, cover and chill until ready to assemble, up to 24 hours.) Wrap cheese cubes with prosciutto strips, and wrap shrimp around cubes, securing with wooden picks. Cover shrimp, and chill 10 minutes.

Whisk together ½ cup olive oil and remaining 3 ingredients in a large bowl. (To make ahead, cover and chill until ready to assemble, up to 24 hours.) Add shrimp, and toss. Cover and chill 10 minutes.

Remove shrimp from marinade, discarding marinade. Yield: 2 dozen.

SMOKED SALMON CANAPÉS

Pair these upscale, open-faced sandwiches with Pinot Noir. It complements salmon well.

1 French baguette
8 ounces thinly sliced smoked salmon
1 (8-ounce) package cream cheese, softened
½ cup sour cream
24 fresh dill sprigs

Cut baguette into 24 (½-inch-thick) slices, and place on a baking sheet.

Bake at 400° for 5 minutes or until lightly toasted; remove slices to wire racks to cool.

Cut salmon into 24 pieces. Spread baguette slices evenly with cream cheese, and top evenly with salmon and sour cream. Place a dill sprig on each canapé. Yield: 2 dozen.

SAVORY PETITS FOURS

Prepare several fillings ahead, and store them in covered containers in the refrigerator.
Select an assortment of breads, and slice the sandwiches into various shapes
to add an element of interest on serving trays.

1 recipe filling (see recipes on pages 72-73)
18 thin white or whole wheat bread slices*
½ cup whipped cream cheese
Garnishes: see filling recipes

Spread about ¼ cup filling on each of 6 bread slices. Top each with another bread slice, and spread with another ¼ cup filling. Top with remaining bread slices. Trim crusts; cut sandwiches into fourths.

Spoon cream cheese into a heavy-duty zip-top plastic bag. Snip a tiny hole in 1 corner of bag, and pipe dollops of cream cheese onto sandwiches. Garnish, if desired. Store sandwiches covered with a damp paper towel in an airtight container in the refrigerator. Yield: 2 dozen.

*36 party rye or pumpernickel bread slices may be substituted for thinly sliced white or whole wheat bread. Spread 2 tablespoons filling between bread slices, and cut sandwiches in half diagonally.

Note: We used Pepperidge Farm Very Thin Sliced White or Wheat Bread. The recipe for "Eggstra" Special Chicken Salad on page 57 may also be used as a spread. Garnish: fresh strawberry wedges with tops

TURKEY-WATERCRESS-AND-CRANBERRY FILLING

2½ cups diced cooked turkey
¾ cup diced dried cranberries
1 bunch fresh watercress, torn
1 (8-ounce) package cream cheese, softened
½ teaspoon seasoned salt
¼ teaspoon freshly ground pepper
Garnishes: fresh watercress leaves, dried
    cranberries

Stir together first 6 ingredients. Serve as a sandwich spread. Garnish, if desired. Yield: about 3 cups.

FRESH ASPARAGUS FILLING

2 pounds thin fresh asparagus
2 (6.5-ounce) containers garlic-and-herbs
    spreadable cheese
2 tablespoons chopped fresh basil
¼ teaspoon freshly ground pepper

Snap off tough ends of asparagus. Cook asparagus in boiling water 3 minutes or until crisp-tender.

Plunge asparagus into ice water to stop the cooking process; drain. Cut 24 (½-inch) tips from asparagus, and cut tips in half lengthwise. Dice remaining asparagus.

Combine diced asparagus, garlic-and-herbs cheese, basil, and pepper. Serve as a sandwich spread. Garnish with asparagus tips. Yield: about 3 cups.

Note: We used Alouette Garlic and Herbs Spreadable Cheese.

SHERRIED SHRIMP FILLING

2 pounds unpeeled, small fresh shrimp
1 (3-ounce) package shrimp, crawfish, and
　　crab boil
1 (4-ounce) package crumbled blue cheese,
　　softened
½ (8-ounce) package cream cheese,
　　softened
¼ cup sherry
5 green onions, minced
½ cup diced celery
½ cup finely chopped walnuts, toasted
½ teaspoon seasoned salt
¼ teaspoon ground red pepper
Garnish: fresh parsley leaves

　　Cook shrimp and package of shrimp,
crawfish, and crab boil according to package
directions; drain.
　　Peel shrimp, and devein, if desired. Set
aside 24 shrimp, and chop remaining shrimp.
　　Stir together chopped shrimp, blue cheese,
and next 7 ingredients. Serve as a sandwich
spread. Garnish with reserved shrimp and, if
desired, parsley leaves. Yield: about 3 cups.
　　Note: We used Zatarain's Boil in Bag
Shrimp, Crawfish, and Crab Boil.

SMOKED SALMON FILLING

3 (8-ounce) packages cream cheese,
　　softened
¾ teaspoon seasoned salt
¼ teaspoon freshly ground pepper
1½ tablespoons fresh dill, minced
2 teaspoons grated lemon rind
6 ounces thinly sliced smoked salmon,
　　divided
Garnish: fresh dill sprigs

　　Stir together first 5 ingredients.
　　Finely chop 4 ounces salmon, and stir
into cream cheese mixture. Cut remaining 2
ounces salmon into ¼-inch-wide strips, and
roll into pinwheels. Serve as a sandwich
spread. Garnish with salmon pinwheels, and,
if desired, dill sprigs. Yield: about 3 cups.

BEST-DRESSED BERRIES

1 (6-ounce) package white chocolate
   baking squares
24 large fresh strawberries
6 (1-ounce) semisweet chocolate squares

Melt white chocolate squares in a small heavy saucepan over low heat, stirring constantly. Press wooden picks into tops of strawberries. Dip each strawberry into melted chocolate, and place on wax paper-lined baking sheets (photo 1). Chill until firm.

Melt semisweet chocolate in a small heavy saucepan over low heat, stirring constantly. Dip 1 side of each coated strawberry halfway into chocolate; dip half of opposite side, forming a V with chocolate (photo 2). Chill until firm.

Spoon remaining semisweet chocolate into a small heavy-duty zip-top plastic bag; seal. (If necessary, submerge bag in hot water until chocolate is piping consistency.) Prick a tiny

hole in 1 corner of bag with a round wooden pick; pipe a bow tie and 3 buttons onto each strawberry to resemble a tuxedo (photo 3). Chill until chocolate is firm or up to 4 hours. Remove wooden picks. Yield: 2 dozen.

These dressed-up berries aren't difficult to make but they do require 3 separate chilling stages, each at least 1 hour, to help set the chocolate. Start them the morning of the party, and plan to finish them up to 4 hours before serving. Need a quick alternative? Serve fresh, pretty berries for dipping into powdered sugar or chocolate fondue.

1 Press wooden picks into the tops of the strawberries. Dip most of the strawberry into the melted white chocolate, leaving just a bit of strawberry showing at the top.

2 Tilt the strawberry against the side of the dish to help form a V on the front side.

3 Pipe the chocolate buttons and bow tie onto the white portion of the strawberry, using a zip-top bag with a tiny hole in the corner.

MINTED ICED TEA

Pictured on page 36.

4 cups boiling water
4 family-size decaffeinated tea bags
½ cup loosely packed fresh mint leaves
¾ cup sugar
1 (6-ounce) can frozen lemonade
   concentrate, thawed and undiluted
4 cups cold water
Garnishes: lemon slices, fresh mint sprigs

Pour 4 cups boiling water over tea bags and mint leaves. Cover; steep 3 minutes. Discard tea bags and mint. Stir in sugar until dissolved. Stir in concentrate and 4 cups cold water; chill. Serve over ice. Garnish, if desired. Yield: 9 cups.

SUNNY SPRING LEMONADE

It takes just minutes to fix this refreshing party favorite. Pictured on pages 45.

6 cups white grape juice, chilled
1 (12-ounce) can frozen lemonade
    concentrate, thawed and undiluted
5½ cups club soda, chilled
Garnish: fresh lemon slices

Stir together all ingredients in a 1-gallon pitcher or punch bowl. Serve over ice. Garnish, if desired. Yield: 12 cups.

MOCK MARGARITAS

Part of the fun of this festive drink is preparing the glasses—spin the rims in salt. Pictured on page 30.

1 (12-ounce) can frozen lemonade
   concentrate, thawed and undiluted
1 (12-ounce) can frozen limeade
   concentrate, thawed and undiluted
1 cup powdered sugar
6 cups crushed ice
Lime wedges
Coarse salt
1 (1-liter) bottle club soda, chilled

Process half of first 4 ingredients in a blender until smooth. Pour mixture into a 4-quart plastic container. Repeat procedure with remaining half of ingredients. Freeze until firm.

Rub rims of stemmed glasses with lime wedges. Place salt in a saucer; spin rim of each glass in salt.

Remove container from freezer 30 minutes before serving; add club soda, stirring until slushy. Pour into glasses. Yield: about 12 cups.

Margaritas: Stir 1 cup tequila into mixture before freezing.

SPIRITED APPLE CIDER

Dark rum adds depth of flavor to this cider.

12 whole cloves
6 whole allspice
3 (3-inch) cinnamon sticks, broken
1 tablespoon grated orange rind
2 quarts apple cider
1 cup orange juice
1 cup cranberry juice cocktail
1 cup pineapple juice
½ cup dark rum
½ cup apple-flavored brandy

Tie first 4 ingredients in a cheesecloth bag. Combine spice bag and cider in a large Dutch oven. Bring to a boil; reduce heat to medium, and cook 35 minutes or until mixture is reduced to 4 cups.

Discard spice bag; stir in orange juice and remaining ingredients. Simmer over medium heat until heated. Yield: 8 cups.

NO-TIME-TO-COOK APPETIZERS

« »

Need an appetizer in a hurry?

Assemble one of these quick fixes.

No cooking allowed.

CREAM CHEESE DRESS-UP

Dress up a plain block of cream cheese with pepper jellies. For a sweeter taste, serve the cheese with gingersnaps instead of crackers.

TAKE A DIP

You'll be surprised how quickly guests will gravitate toward something as simple as chips and salsa. Look for salsa in decorative jars so you don't need to bother with a bowl.

CHICKEN FINGERS FAST

For a hearty appetizer, chicken fingers are always a favorite. Buy them in the deli section of the grocery store, and add a bowl of honey mustard or another dipping sauce for a tasty treat.

»

JUST CHEESE, PLEASE

«

Many grocery stores have a scrumptious selection of cheese and bread. Choose some different flavors of each, and arrange on a plate or in a basket. Consider adding some grapes, apples, or other fruit to the mix.

the main
event

BAKED HAM WITH BOURBON GLAZE

As it bakes, this succulent ham will whet eager appetites with a smoky, sweet aroma. You can serve the ham and glaze alone for a dressier meal or sandwiched with biscuits for a more casual gathering.

1 (7- to 8-pound) bone-in smoked
   spiral-cut ham half
1 cup honey
½ cup molasses
½ cup bourbon or orange juice
¼ cup orange juice
2 tablespoons Dijon mustard

Remove skin and excess fat from ham; place ham in a greased 13- x 9-inch pan.

Microwave honey and molasses in a 1-quart glass dish at HIGH 1 minute. Whisk to blend. Whisk in bourbon, juice, and mustard. Pour glaze over ham.

Bake ham on lower oven rack at 350° for 2 to 2½ hours or until a meat thermometer inserted into thickest portion registers 140°, basting every 20 minutes with glaze.

Remove ham from pan, reserving drippings. Skim fat from drippings if you'd like to serve drippings alongside ham. Yield: 12 to 15 servings.

PEPPERED BEEF TENDERLOIN

We used less pungent red and green peppercorns for holiday entertaining. You can substitute black peppercorns.
They're hotter, so reduce the amount a little if you'd like.

1 (8-ounce) container sour cream
3 tablespoons Dijon mustard
2 tablespoons prepared horseradish
2 tablespoons whole green peppercorns
2 tablespoons whole red peppercorns
2 teaspoons coarse salt
1 (3½- to 4-pound) beef tenderloin, trimmed
1 cup chopped fresh flat-leaf parsley
¼ cup butter, softened
3 tablespoons Dijon mustard
Garnishes: baby artichokes, fresh rosemary sprigs

Combine first 3 ingredients. Cover and chill. Process peppercorns in a blender until chopped. Transfer to a bowl, and stir in salt.

Place tenderloin on a lightly greased rack in a shallow roasting pan. Combine parsley, butter, and 3 tablespoons mustard; rub mixture evenly over tenderloin. Pat peppercorn mixture evenly over tenderloin. Cover and chill up to 24 hours.

Bake at 350° for 50 minutes or until a meat thermometer inserted in thickest portion registers 145° (medium rare) to 160° (medium). Transfer tenderloin to a platter; cover loosely with aluminum foil. Let stand 10 minutes before slicing. Serve with sour cream mixture. Garnish, if desired. Yield: 8 servings.

ROSEMARY PORK TENDERLOIN

For a sandwich option, serve the tenderloin with rolls and
use the pepper sauce as a spread. Pictured on page 42.

⅔ cup fresh rosemary leaves
5 garlic cloves
⅓ cup olive oil
2 tablespoons kosher salt
½ teaspoon pepper
4 (¾-pound) pork tenderloins,
    trimmed
Garnish: fresh rosemary sprigs
Roasted Red Pepper Sauce

Process rosemary and garlic in a food
processor until smooth, stopping to scrape
down sides. With processor running, pour oil
through food chute in a slow, steady stream.
Add kosher salt and pepper; pulse until
blended.

Spread rosemary pesto evenly over tenderloins. Place tenderloins on a lightly greased
rack in a broiler pan. (Cover and chill
overnight, if desired.)

Bake, uncovered, at 350° for 40 minutes
or until a meat thermometer inserted into
thickest portion registers 160°. Let stand 10
minutes before slicing. Garnish, if desired.
Serve with Roasted Red Pepper Sauce. Yield:
8 to 10 servings.

ROASTED RED PEPPER SAUCE

1 (12-ounce) jar roasted sweet red
    peppers, drained
20 kalamata olives, pitted
½ cup lemon juice
2 tablespoons balsamic vinegar
2 teaspoons capers
2 teaspoons anchovy paste
3 tablespoons olive oil
½ teaspoon salt
½ teaspoon pepper

Process first 6 ingredients in a food
processor or blender until mixture is smooth.
With processor running, pour olive oil
through food chute in a slow, steady stream.
Add salt and pepper; pulse until blended.
Yield: 2 cups.

ITALIAN PORK ROAST

Garlic slices infuse further flavor into this roast rubbed with Italian seasoning.

1 (3- to 3½ pound) boneless pork loin
  roast
2 large garlic cloves, cut into 4 slices each
1 tablespoon olive oil
2 tablespoons dried Italian seasoning
1½ teaspoons coarsely ground pepper
Garnish: fresh herbs

Place roast, fat side up, on a rack in a shallow roasting pan. Cut 8 small slits in roast at 2-inch intervals; insert garlic deep into slits.

Brush oil evenly over roast. Combine Italian seasoning and pepper; rub over entire surface of roast. Bake, uncovered, at 325° for 1 hour and 20 minutes or until a meat thermometer inserted in thickest portion registers 160° (medium). Let stand 10 to 15 minutes before slicing. Garnish, if desired. Yield: 10 servings.

CHICKEN ENCHILADA CASSEROLE

This casserole is hearty enough to serve on its own, but Mexican rice would be a tasty side.

1¼ pounds skinned and boned chicken
   breast halves
2 tablespoons olive oil, divided
1 large onion, chopped
4 garlic cloves, minced
¼ teaspoon ground red pepper
2 (14½-ounce) cans Mexican stewed
   tomatoes
2 (4.5-ounce) cans chopped green chiles
½ cup butter or margarine
⅓ cup all-purpose flour
2 tablespoons fajita seasoning
2 cups half-and-half
9 (5-inch) corn tortillas, cut in half
1 (8-ounce) package shredded Mexican
   cheese blend
Toppings: sliced green onions, sliced ripe
   olives, salsa, sour cream

Cook chicken in 1 tablespoon hot oil in a large skillet over medium-high heat 6 minutes on each side or until done. Remove from pan; cool and shred chicken.

Sauté onion and garlic in remaining 1 tablespoon hot oil until tender. Add red pepper and tomatoes; cook, stirring occasionally, 10 minutes or until most of liquid evaporates. Remove from heat, and stir in chicken and green chiles.

Melt butter in a heavy saucepan over low heat; whisk in flour and fajita seasoning until mixture is smooth. Cook, whisking constantly, 1 minute. Gradually whisk in half-and-half, and cook over medium heat, whisking constantly, until mixture is thickened and bubbly.

Spread ½ cup white sauce in a lightly greased 13- x 9-inch baking dish. Arrange 6 tortilla halves over sauce. Top with half of chicken mixture and ⅔ cup shredded cheese. Repeat layers once. Spoon ½ cup sauce over cheese; top with remaining tortilla halves. Spoon remaining sauce over tortillas. Reserve remaining cheese.

Cover and bake at 350° for 40 minutes or until thoroughly heated. Sprinkle with remaining cheese, and let stand 10 minutes. Serve with desired toppings. Yield: 8 servings.

SAUCY MANICOTTI

A salad is all you need to put together a dinner for a group. Pictured on page 39.

¾ pound hot Italian sausage
¾ pound ground chuck
1 large onion, chopped
5 garlic cloves, pressed
2 (15-ounce) cans tomato sauce
1 (14½-ounce) can diced tomatoes, undrained
1 (6-ounce) can tomato paste
1 tablespoon dried Italian seasoning
1 (8-ounce) package manicotti shells
1 (8-ounce) container cream cheese with chives and onions, softened
5 cups (20 ounces) shredded mozzarella cheese, divided
¾ cup shredded Parmesan cheese
1 (15-ounce) container ricotta cheese
4 garlic cloves, pressed
¾ teaspoon pepper
Garnishes: chopped fresh parsley, shredded Parmesan cheese

Remove and discard casings from sausage. Cook sausage, beef, onion, and garlic in a large Dutch oven over medium heat, stirring until sausage and beef crumble and are no longer pink; drain. Return sausage mixture to Dutch oven.

Stir in tomato sauce and next 3 ingredients; bring to a boil. Cover, reduce heat, and simmer, stirring occasionally, 30 minutes.

While sauce simmers, cook pasta shells according to package directions.

Stir together cream cheese, 4 cups mozzarella cheese, and next 4 ingredients. Stuff evenly into shells.

Spoon half of sauce evenly into 2 greased 13- x 9-inch baking dishes. Arrange stuffed shells over sauce; top with remaining sauce.

Cover and bake at 350° for 30 minutes or until thoroughly heated. Uncover and sprinkle with remaining 1 cup mozzarella cheese. Bake 10 more minutes or until cheese melts. Let stand 5 minutes before serving. Garnish, if desired. Yield: 7 servings.

Note: Casserole may be frozen. Thaw in refrigerator 12 hours. Cover and bake at 350° for 45 to 50 minutes or until thoroughly heated. Uncover and sprinkle with remaining 1 cup mozzarella cheese, and bake 10 more minutes or until cheese melts. Let stand 5 minutes.

BARBECUE BURGER CASSEROLE

This is a great casserole for the kids—actually, for the kid in all of us.

2 pounds ground chuck
1 medium onion, chopped
¾ cup barbecue sauce
¾ cup spicy ketchup
1 tablespoon prepared mustard
1 teaspoon salt
1 teaspoon pepper
1 (8-ounce) package cream cheese, softened
1 (8-ounce) container sour cream
¾ cup chopped green onions
3 cups hot cooked medium egg noodles
2½ cups (10 ounces) shredded Cheddar or
   American cheese, divided
Garnish: chopped dill pickle

Cook ground chuck and onion in a large skillet over medium heat, stirring until beef crumbles and is no longer pink. Drain and return to skillet.

Add barbecue sauce and next 4 ingredients to beef mixture. Bring to a boil; cover, reduce heat, and simmer 10 minutes, stirring once.

Combine cream cheese and sour cream, stirring until smooth. Stir in green onions and cooked noodles.

Layer half of noodle mixture in a greased 13- x 9-inch baking dish. Top with half of beef mixture. Sprinkle with 1 cup cheese. Top with remaining noodle mixture and remaining beef mixture. (If desired, cover and chill overnight. Let stand at room temperature 30 minutes before baking.)

Cover and bake at 350° for 30 minutes or until thoroughly heated. Uncover and sprinkle with remaining 1½ cups cheese; bake 5 more minutes. Garnish, if desired. Yield: 8 servings.

RICH SEAFOOD CASSEROLE

Fresh shrimp and scallops come to the table baked in a
Swiss cheese and wine sauce just right for spooning over rice.

1½ pounds unpeeled, large fresh shrimp
1½ cups dry white wine
¼ cup chopped onion
¼ cup fresh parsley sprigs or celery leaves
1 tablespoon butter or margarine
1 teaspoon salt
1 pound bay scallops
3 tablespoons butter or margarine
3 tablespoons all-purpose flour
1 cup half-and-half
½ cup (2 ounces) shredded Swiss cheese
1 tablespoon lemon juice
¼ teaspoon lemon pepper
1 (7-ounce) can sliced mushrooms, drained
1 cup soft whole wheat breadcrumbs
¼ cup grated Parmesan cheese
¼ cup sliced almonds
2 tablespoons butter or margarine, melted
Hot cooked rice

Peel shrimp and devein, if desired; set aside.

Combine wine and next 4 ingredients in a Dutch oven; bring to a boil. Add shrimp and scallops; cook 3 to 5 minutes or until shrimp turn pink. Drain shrimp mixture, reserving ⅔ cup broth.

Melt 3 tablespoons butter in Dutch oven over low heat; add flour, stirring until smooth. Cook, stirring constantly, 1 minute. Gradually add half-and-half; cook over medium heat, stirring constantly, until mixture is thickened and bubbly.

Add Swiss cheese to sauce, stirring until cheese melts. Gradually stir in reserved ⅔ cup broth, lemon juice, and lemon pepper. Stir in shrimp mixture and mushrooms.

Spoon mixture into a lightly greased 11- x 7-inch baking dish. (If desired, cover and chill overnight. Let stand at room temperature 30 minutes before baking.)

Cover and bake at 350° for 40 minutes. Combine breadcrumbs and next 3 ingredients; sprinkle over casserole. Bake, uncovered, 10 minutes. Let stand 10 minutes before serving. Serve over hot cooked rice. Yield: 8 servings.

SHERRIED CHICKEN-AND-GRAPE SALAD

Serve this salad over a melon wedge or lettuce. Either way, it's sure to get rave reviews.
Pictured on page 44.

6 cups chopped cooked chicken
3 cups sliced green grapes
1 cup toasted slivered almonds
2 celery ribs, diced
3 green onions, minced
¾ cup mayonnaise
¼ cup sour cream
2 tablespoons sherry
½ teaspoon seasoned salt
½ teaspoon seasoned pepper

Stir all ingredients together. Cover and chill salad until ready to serve. Yield: 6 to 8 servings.

BLACK BEAN WRAPS

For a festive touch, tie these sandwiches with ribbon in your team's colors. Pictured on page 28.

2 (8-ounce) packages cream cheese, softened
2 cups (8 ounces) shredded Monterey Jack
   cheese with peppers
½ cup sour cream
1 teaspoon onion salt
2 (15-ounce) cans black beans, rinsed and
   drained
¼ cup salsa
12 (8-inch) flour tortillas
1 (10-ounce) package fresh spinach
2 (7-ounce) jars roasted sweet red peppers,
   drained and coarsely chopped
2 carrots, shredded (optional)

Beat first 4 ingredients in a large bowl at medium speed with an electric mixer until thoroughly blended. Set cheese mixture aside.

Process beans and salsa in a food processor until smooth, stopping to scrape down sides.

Spread bean mixture evenly over tortillas; top each evenly with cheese mixture, spinach, peppers, and, if desired, carrot. Roll tortillas tightly; wrap each in plastic wrap. Chill, if desired. Serve with salsa. Yield: 12 servings.

Note: The cheese mixture and bean mixture can be prepared a day ahead, but assemble the wraps no more than 4 hours ahead. Cover and chill until ready to serve.

NO-TIME-TO-COOK ENTRÉES

‹‹ ››

If you want to host a dinner party, but wince at the thought of cooking for a crowd, try one of these easy entrées.

SANDWICH SUPPER

‹‹ Order a meat and cheese tray from the grocery store or deli. Add some focaccia or rolls so your guests can create their own sandwiches.

FAJITA NIGHT

For an instant fiesta, just heat and serve a package of frozen fajita chicken or steak—some even come with chopped vegetables and tortillas. Add bowls filled with store-bought salsa and guacamole, shredded cheese, and sour cream.

YOUR-OWN-DISH TRICK

Take your own dish to a gourmet take-out shop so they can make a casserole in it. Simply heat the casserole in the oven before your guests arrive.

NOODLE ON THIS

Some Italian restaurants sell containers of their spaghetti sauce and sometimes even fresh pasta, salad, and garlic bread to serve on the side. Just call ahead to reserve.

on the
side

RICE SALAD WITH ORANGE VINAIGRETTE

A balsamic vinaigrette stands up nicely to the rustic wild and brown rice combo in this rice salad.

4¼ cups water
⅔ cup uncooked wild rice*
1⅓ cups uncooked brown rice*
½ cup chopped pecans, toasted
6 green onions, chopped
¼ cup minced fresh parsley
2 tablespoons butter or margarine
½ teaspoon salt
½ teaspoon pepper
Orange Vinaigrette
Garnishes: orange wedges, fresh parsley
   sprigs

Bring water to a boil in a saucepan; add wild rice. Reduce heat; simmer 15 minutes. Stir in brown rice; cover. Simmer 30 minutes or until liquid is absorbed.

Stir in pecans and next 5 ingredients. Toss with Orange Vinaigrette. Transfer to a bowl; cover and chill 2 hours. Garnish, if desired. Yield: 5 cups.

* Substitute 2 (6-ounce) packages long-grain and wild rice mix for wild rice and brown rice, if desired. Omit 4½ cups water; prepare mix according to package directions.

ORANGE VINAIGRETTE

½ cup olive oil
¼ cup white balsamic vinegar*
1 tablespoon grated orange rind
⅓ cup fresh orange juice
2 garlic cloves

Process all ingredients in a blender until smooth. Yield: 1 cup.

* Substitute ¼ cup white wine vinegar for white balsamic vinegar, if desired.

FRESH FRUIT WITH CELERY-POPPY SEED DRESSING

No time to cut up fruit? Buy it from the deli or supermarket salad bar. Toss the fruit with lemon juice to keep it looking fresh. Bottled poppy seed dressing speeds up prep when you're in a pinch. Pictured on page 35.

⅔ cup sugar
⅓ cup honey
5 tablespoons white vinegar
1 tablespoon fresh lemon juice
1 teaspoon dry mustard
1 teaspoon paprika
1 teaspoon celery seed
1 teaspoon poppy seed
¼ teaspoon salt
1 cup vegetable oil
8 cups assorted fruit (melon cubes, strawberry halves, pineapple chunks, kiwi slices)

Process first 9 ingredients in a blender until smooth, stopping to scrape down sides. With blender running, add oil in a slow, steady stream. Chill 8 hours, if desired. Serve with assorted fruit. Yield: 12 to 15 servings.

SPINACH SALAD WITH HOT CITRUS DRESSING

2 (6-ounce) packages fresh baby spinach
4 oranges, peeled and sectioned
1 large purple onion, thinly sliced and
    separated into rings
3 ounces goat cheese, crumbled
1 cup sweetened dried cranberries
½ cup chopped pecans, toasted
Hot Citrus Dressing

Arrange spinach and next 5 ingredients on 8 salad plates. Drizzle with Hot Citrus Dressing. Yield: 8 servings.

HOT CITRUS DRESSING

1 (6-ounce) can frozen orange juice
    concentrate, thawed
1 small onion, diced
⅓ cup red wine vinegar
1 cup firmly packed light brown sugar
1 tablespoon grated orange rind
1 teaspoon dry mustard
1 teaspoon salt
1 teaspoon hot sauce
1 cup peanut oil

Process first 3 ingredients in a blender until smooth. Add brown sugar and next 4 ingredients; process until smooth. Turn blender on high; add oil in a slow, steady stream.

Bring dressing to a boil in a medium-size nonaluminum saucepan. Cook over medium heat 10 minutes. Yield: 2½ cups.

SWEET 'N' HOT GREEN BEANS AND CARROTS

Mix the vinaigrette a day ahead, and wash and prepare the veggies, bagging them separately.
Pour the vinaigrette over the veggies about an hour before serving so they'll absorb flavor.
Marinating longer gives them even more flavor, but dulls their bright colors. Pictured on page 28.

1 cup sugar
1 cup white wine vinegar
½ to 1 teaspoon dried crushed red pepper
2 garlic cloves, minced
1 pound small fresh green beans, trimmed
1 pound carrots, cut into 4- x ½-inch
   strips

Whisk together sugar and vinegar until sugar dissolves. Stir in red pepper and garlic; cover and let stand 4 hours.

Cook green beans and carrots in boiling water 1 minute; drain. Plunge into ice water to stop cooking process; drain.

Pour vinegar mixture over vegetables, tossing to coat. Let stand 1 hour before serving. Yield: 6 to 8 servings.

GREEN BEAN BUNDLES

The most obvious time-saver in this recipe is to omit the bundling. You can also use frozen green beans to eliminate the time spent trimming fresh ones.

3 quarts water
1 ½ pounds fresh green beans
1 large carrot, scraped
¼ cup butter or margarine
½ teaspoon garlic powder
¼ teaspoon dried basil
¼ teaspoon hot sauce
2 tablespoons diced pimiento (optional)
2 teaspoons finely grated lemon rind

Bring 3 quarts water to a boil in a Dutch oven. Meanwhile, wash beans; trim ends, and remove strings. Set beans aside.

Cut off and discard ½ inch from each end of carrot. Using a vegetable peeler, cut 8 paper-thin lengthwise strips from carrot; trim ends evenly. Add carrot strips to boiling water in Dutch oven; cook 45 seconds or just until tender. Remove with a slotted spoon; set aside, and cool.

Return water to a boil, and add beans. Cook 5 minutes or until crisp-tender. Drain; rinse with cold water, and drain. Gather 8 to 12 cooked beans into a bundle; wrap 1 carrot strip around each bundle. Tie ends in a knot or tuck ends under each bundle, and place in a large shallow baking dish.

Melt butter in a small skillet over medium heat. Stir in garlic powder, basil, and hot sauce; cook 30 seconds. Drizzle melted butter mixture over beans. Cover with aluminum foil, and chill up to 1 day.

When ready to serve, cover and bake beans at 350° for 10 minutes or until thoroughly heated. Sprinkle with pimiento, if desired, and lemon rind before serving. Serve carefully, keeping bundles wrapped with carrot strips. Yield: 8 servings.

ROASTED VEGETABLES

Roasting brings out the natural sweetness in vegetables. High heat caramelizes the surface and seals in flavor.
Scatter these colorful roasted chunks on a serving platter with your choice of entrée.

1½ pounds sweet potatoes (2 medium),
     peeled and cut into 1½-inch pieces
¾ pound turnips (3 small), peeled and cut
     into 1½-inch pieces
1 large onion, peeled and cut into 1½-inch
     wedges
6 garlic cloves, peeled
3 tablespoons olive oil
1 tablespoon chopped fresh rosemary
1 tablespoon chopped fresh oregano or
     marjoram
1 teaspoon salt

Combine first 5 ingredients in a large bowl; toss well. Arrange vegetables in a single layer in a large roasting pan or broiler pan. Roast at 450° for 25 to 30 minutes or until well browned, stirring gently every 10 minutes. Stir in herbs and salt just before serving. Yield: 6 servings.

GLAZED ONIONS

You can save time by purchasing frozen pearl onions and skipping the blanching process for fresh onions.

2 **pounds white or red pearl onions, peeled (about 4 cups)* or 1 (16-ounce) bag frozen pearl onions**
⅓ **cup butter or margarine**
½ **cup firmly packed brown sugar**
⅓ **cup light corn syrup**
½ **teaspoon salt**
1 **tablespoon chopped fresh parsley (optional)**

Arrange onions in a steamer basket over boiling water; cover and steam 10 minutes or until tender. Place in a lightly greased 8-inch square baking dish.

Melt butter in a small saucepan over medium-low heat. Add sugar, corn syrup, and salt; bring to a boil over medium heat. Reduce heat; simmer 5 minutes. Pour over onions.

Cover and bake at 350° for 25 minutes.

Remove from oven, and cool. Cover with aluminum foil, and chill overnight.

Remove aluminum foil from baking dish; cover dish tightly with heavy-duty plastic wrap. Fold back a small edge (or corner) of wrap to allow steam to escape.

Microwave at MEDIUM (50% power) 12 minutes or until thoroughly heated, turning dish once. Sprinkle with parsley, if desired. Yield: 8 servings.

* A quick and easy way to peel pearl onions is to trim bottom ends of onions and blanch onions in bunches for about 45 seconds in rapidly boiling water. (It's important to blanch in batches so that the water remains at a boil.) Drain onions, and immediately place in a bowl of ice water to stop the cooking process. Simply squeeze trimmed end of each onion gently, and the skins will slide right off.

BROCCOLI AND CAULIFLOWER GRATIN

2 (16-ounce) packages fresh broccoli and
   cauliflower florets
1½ cups reduced-fat mayonnaise
1 cup (4 ounces) shredded Cheddar cheese
1 (3-ounce) package shredded Parmesan
   cheese
4 green onions, sliced
2 tablespoons Dijon mustard
¼ teaspoon ground red pepper
3 tablespoons Italian-seasoned
   breadcrumbs

Arrange florets in a steamer basket over boiling water. Cover and steam 6 to 8 minutes or until crisp-tender. Drain well.

Arrange florets in a lightly greased 2-quart baking dish.

Stir together mayonnaise and next 5 ingredients. Spoon over florets. Sprinkle with breadcrumbs.

Bake at 350° for 20 to 25 minutes or until breadcrumbs are golden. Yield: 8 servings.

SMOKY SCALLOPED POTATOES

1 garlic clove, minced
1 cup whipping cream
1 cup milk
1½ tablespoons all-purpose flour
2 teaspoons adobo sauce
1 teaspoon mashed chipotle pepper
¼ teaspoon salt
¼ teaspoon pepper
2 medium-size sweet potatoes, peeled and
     thinly sliced
1 medium-size baking potato, peeled and
     thinly sliced

Sprinkle garlic in a buttered 11- x 7-inch baking dish.

Whisk together whipping cream and next 6 ingredients.

Layer half of potato slices over garlic; top with half of cream mixture. Repeat procedure with remaining potato slices and cream mixture.

Cover and bake at 350° for 40 minutes. Uncover and bake 30 more minutes or until gratin is golden brown. Let stand 15 minutes before serving. Yield: 6 to 8 servings.

Note: For testing purposes we used canned chipotle peppers in adobo sauce. They may be found in the ethnic food section of the grocery store.

TWICE-BAKED POTATO CASSEROLE

Here's how to create a great-looking garnish: Cut 2-inch-wide strips of wax paper, and arrange on top of casserole. Then sprinkle the uncovered areas with cheese. Next, remove the paper, and sprinkle remaining areas with chives and bacon.

8 medium-size baking potatoes (4 pounds), baked
2 cups (8 ounces) shredded Cheddar cheese, divided
1 (16-ounce) container sour cream
1 (8-ounce) package cream cheese, softened
½ cup milk
½ cup butter or margarine, melted
2 garlic cloves, minced
1 tablespoon chopped fresh chives
1½ teaspoons salt
½ teaspoon pepper
6 bacon slices, cooked and crumbled
¼ cup chopped fresh chives
Garnish: chive bundles

Peel potatoes, and coarsely mash pulp with a potato masher. Stir in 1 cup Cheddar cheese, sour cream, and next 7 ingredients. Spoon into a lightly greased 13- x 9-inch baking dish.

Bake at 350° for 30 minutes or until thoroughly heated. Sprinkle with remaining 1 cup cheese, bacon, and chives. Garnish, if desired. Yield: 8 servings.

NO-TIME-TO-COOK
SALADS

《 》

For a salad with minimal assembly, take

advantage of bottled dressings and precut

fruits and vegetables.

SALAD BY THE POUND

Hit the grocery store salad bar for a

variety of fresh salad greens, vegetables,

and fruits that are already washed and

《 cut. Package the produce separately, or

mix the salad on the spot, all for one

price per pound. Add bottled dressings,

and the salad's ready.

FRUIT IN A FLASH

Most grocery store produce sections have containers of precut fruits. Add a tangy-sweet dressing for a quick dish.

«

IT'S IN THE BAG

Try prepackaged salads that usually can be found near the lettuce. They contain everything you need—even the dressing and croutons.

»

3-BEAN SALAD SAVVY

For an instant marinated salad, drain and mix 1 can of green beans, 1 can of lima beans, and 1 can of kidney beans with a bottled vinaigrette. Garnish with cherry tomatoes.

«

the grande finale

CHEWY ALMOND-FUDGE BARS

Coconut candy bars and toasted almonds give these brownies personality.
If you like firm bars, chill them.

1 (19.8-ounce) package chewy fudge
    brownie mix
3 tablespoons vegetable oil
1 cup sweetened condensed milk
14 miniature dark chocolate coconut candy
    bars, chopped (1 ¼ cups)
¾ cup chopped natural almonds, toasted

Prepare brownie mix according to package directions, reducing vegetable oil to 3 table-spoons; pour batter into a lightly greased 13- x 9-inch pan. Pour sweetened condensed milk over batter; sprinkle with chopped candy bars and almonds.

Bake at 350° for 36 to 38 minutes. Cool completely in pan on a wire rack. Cut into bars. Yield: 2 dozen.

Note: For brownie mix, we used Duncan Hines. For miniature dark chocolate coconut candy bars, we used Mounds.

CARAMEL-WALNUT BROWNIES

These brownies are so luscious and gooey. If you plan to nibble on them warm, you'll need a fork!
Chill them if you'd like them firmer.

1 (14-ounce) package caramels
⅔ cup evaporated milk, divided
1 (18.25-ounce) package caramel-flavored
   cake mix
¾ cup butter or margarine, melted
2 teaspoons vanilla extract
¾ teaspoon ground cinnamon
1½ cups walnut halves or pieces

Unwrap caramels, and place in a medium saucepan. Add ⅓ cup evaporated milk; cook over low heat until caramels melt, stirring often. Remove from heat, and set aside.

Combine remaining ⅓ cup milk, cake mix, and next 3 ingredients; stir just until blended. Spread half of dough into a lightly greased 9-inch square pan. (Remaining dough will stiffen as it sits.) Bake at 350° for 10 minutes. Cool in pan on a wire rack 5 minutes.

Pour caramel mixture over brownie layer in pan. Sprinkle with walnuts.

Divide remaining half of dough into 6 portions. Shape each portion into a 4-inch circle. Place circles over walnuts in pan, overlapping slightly. (Dough will spread during baking.)

Bake at 350° for 25 minutes. Cool completely in pan on wire rack. Cover and chill brownies thoroughly before cutting. Yield: 15 brownies.

Note: For caramel-flavored cake mix, we used Duncan Hines.

SEVEN-LAYER SQUARES

Don't miss the white chocolate variation on these indulgent squares.
You'll enjoy them with or without cinnamon.

⅓ cup butter or margarine
1½ cups graham cracker crumbs
1 cup flaked coconut
1 cup (6 ounces) semisweet chocolate
    morsels
1 cup (6 ounces) butterscotch morsels
1 cup chopped pecans
1 (14-ounce) can sweetened condensed
    milk

Place butter in a 9-inch square pan, and bake at 325° for 3 minutes or until melted.

Layer graham cracker crumbs, coconut, chocolate morsels, butterscotch morsels, and pecans in pan with melted butter. (Do not stir.) Spread condensed milk evenly over top.

Bake at 325° for 33 minutes. Cool completely in pan. Cut into 1½-inch squares. Yield: 3 dozen.

White Chocolate-Cinnamon Layer Squares: Stir 2 teaspoons ground cinnamon into graham cracker crumbs before layering crumbs in pan. Substitute 1 cup chopped white chocolate for butterscotch morsels.

SHORTBREAD COOKIE HEARTS

These cookies are great to make ahead; you can freeze them up to 3 weeks.

1 cup butter, softened
⅔ cup sugar
1 egg yolk
2 teaspoons vanilla extract
2 cups all-purpose flour
⅛ teaspoon salt
1 large egg
1 tablespoon water
White sparkling sugar

Beat butter at medium speed with an electric mixer until creamy. Gradually add ⅔ cup sugar, beating well. Add egg yolk and vanilla extract beat 1 minute.

Combine flour and salt; gradually add to butter mixture, beating mixture at low speed just until blended. Beat at medium speed 2 minutes.

Divide dough into 3 portions; wrap individually in plastic wrap, and chill 8 hours.

Line 3 baking sheets with parchment paper. Sprinkle each lightly with flour.

Unwrap 1 dough portion, and roll on a lightly floured surface to ¼-inch thickness. Cut into heart shapes, using a 2-inch cookie cutter. Place on prepared baking sheet.

Whisk together egg and 1 tablespoon water; brush over cookies. Sprinkle with sparkling sugar. Repeat procedure with remaining dough, rerolling scraps, if desired.

Bake at 350° for 8 to 10 minutes or until lightly browned; cool on baking sheet 10 minutes. Transfer to wire racks to cool completely. Freeze up to 3 weeks, if desired. Serve cookie hearts with your favorite ice cream or sherbet and strawberries, if desired. Yield: 5 dozen.

SATINY MOCHA TORTE

Convenience products do most of the work in this stunning four-layer cake with a shiny chocolate top.

1 (18.25-ounce) package devil's food cake
   mix without pudding
2 (2.8-ounce) packages mocha mousse mix
1⅓ cups milk
¾ cup whipping cream
1½ tablespoons Swiss-style flavored
   instant coffee powder
6 (1-ounce) squares semisweet chocolate,
   chopped
¾ cup chopped hazelnuts
Garnish: strawberry slices

Grease and flour 2 (9-inch) cakepans. Prepare cake mix according to package directions; pour into prepared pans. Bake at 350° for 30 minutes or until a wooden pick inserted in center comes out clean. Cool in pans on wire racks 15 minutes; remove from pans, and cool completely on wire racks.

Prepare mousse mix according to package directions, using 1⅓ cups milk; cover and chill.

Split cake layers in half horizontally to make 4 layers. Place 1 layer on a serving plate; place 4 strips of wax paper under and around cake layer. Spread one-third of mousse over layer. Repeat procedure with second and third layers and remaining mousse. Top stack with fourth layer. Chill 30 minutes.

Combine whipping cream and coffee powder in a saucepan; bring to a simmer over medium heat. Remove from heat; add chocolate. Let stand 1 minute. Stir until chocolate melts. Cool 30 minutes.

Pour chocolate glaze over torte, letting excess drip down sides onto wax paper. Using a small spatula, smooth excess glaze onto sides of torte. Gently press hazelnuts onto sides of glazed torte. Carefully pull wax paper strips from beneath torte. Store in refrigerator. Garnish, if desired. Yield: 1 (9-inch) torte.

Note: We used Duncan Hines devil's food cake mix, Nestlé mocha mousse mixes, and General Foods International Coffees Suisse Mocha.

OLD-FASHIONED POUND CAKE

We recommend real butter for this moist pound cake. There's just no substitute.

2 cups butter, softened
2¾ cups sugar
6 large eggs
3¾ cups all-purpose flour
⅛ teaspoon salt
¼ teaspoon ground nutmeg
½ cup milk
1 teaspoon vanilla extract

Beat butter at medium speed with an electric mixer 2 minutes or until creamy. Gradually add sugar, beating 5 to 7 minutes. Add eggs, 1 at a time, beating just until yellow disappears.

Combine flour, salt, and nutmeg in a large bowl; add to butter mixture alternately with milk, beginning and ending with flour mixture.

Mix at low speed after each addition just until mixture is blended. Stir in vanilla. Spoon batter into a greased and floured 10-inch tube pan.

Bake at 325° for 1 hour and 15 to 20 minutes or until a wooden pick inserted in center comes out clean. Cool in pan on a wire rack 10 to 15 minutes; remove from pan, and cool completely on wire rack. Yield: 14 servings.

ITALIAN CREAM CAKE

1 cup butter or margarine, softened
2 cups sugar
5 large eggs, separated
2½ cups all-purpose flour
1 teaspoon baking soda
1 cup buttermilk
⅔ cup finely chopped pecans
1 teaspoon vanilla extract
1 (3½-ounce) can flaked coconut
½ teaspoon cream of tartar
3 tablespoons light rum
Cream Cheese Frosting

Grease and flour 3 (9-inch) round cakepans. Line pans with wax paper; grease paper, and set pans aside.

Beat butter at medium speed with an electric mixer until creamy; gradually add sugar, beating well. Add egg yolks, 1 at a time, beating after each addition. Combine flour and baking soda.; add to butter mixture alternately with buttermilk, beginning and ending with flour mixture. Stir in pecans, vanilla, and coconut.

Beat egg whites at high speed in a large bowl until foamy. Add cream of tartar, and beat until stiff peaks form. Gently fold beaten egg whites into batter. Pour batter into prepared pans.

Bake at 350° for 25 to 30 minutes or until a wooden pick inserted in center comes out clean. Cool in pans 10 minutes. Remove from pans; peel off wax paper, and cool completely on wire racks. Sprinkle each cake layer with 1 tablespoon light rum. Let stand 10 minutes. Spread Cream Cheese Frosting between layers and on sides and top of cake. Yield: 1 (3-layer) cake.

CREAM CHEESE FROSTING

1 (8-ounce) package cream cheese, softened
1 (3-ounce) package cream cheese, softened
¾ cup butter, softened
1½ (16-ounce) packages powdered sugar, sifted
1½ cups chopped pecans
1 tablespoon vanilla extract

Beat first 3 ingredients at medium speed with an electric mixer until smooth. Gradually add powdered sugar, beating until light and fluffy. Stir in pecans and vanilla. Yield: enough for 1 (3-layer) cake.

CARROT CAKE ROULAGE

Carrot cake claims a new shape in this jellyroll. Look for the lavish cream cheese frosting rolled up inside.

4 large eggs
½ cup water
1 (18.25-ounce) package spice cake mix
1 cup grated carrot
3 tablespoons powdered sugar, divided
1 (15¼-ounce) can crushed pineapple in
   heavy syrup
2 (16-ounce) cans cream cheese frosting
½ cup chopped pecans, toasted
Powdered sugar
Garnish: toasted chopped pecans

Coat 2 (15- x 10-inch) jellyroll pans with vegetable cooking spray; line with wax paper, and coat wax paper with cooking spray.

Beat eggs in a large bowl at medium-high speed with an electric mixer 5 minutes. Add water, beating at low speed until blended. Gradually add cake mix, beating until moistened. Beat mixture at medium-high speed 2 minutes. Fold in grated carrot.

Spread batter evenly in prepared pans. (Layers will be thin.) Bake, 1 at a time or in separate ovens, at 350° on the middle rack 13 minutes or until each cake springs back when lightly touched in center.

Sift 1½ tablespoons powdered sugar in a 15- x 10-inch rectangle on a cloth towel; repeat with 1½ tablespoons sugar and a second towel. When cakes are done, immediately loosen from sides of pans, and turn each out onto a sugared towel. Peel off wax paper. Starting at narrow end, tightly roll up each cake and towel together; place seam side down on wire racks to cool completely.

Drain pineapple, reserving ¼ cup syrup. Press pineapple between paper towels to remove excess moisture. Combine pineapple, cream cheese frosting, and ½ cup pecans; stir well.

Unroll cakes; brush each lightly with 2 tablespoons pineapple syrup. Spread each cake with half of frosting mixture. Reroll cakes without towels; place seam side down on serving plates. Chill at least 1 hour. Dust with additional powdered sugar before serving. Garnish, if desired. Yield: 2 cake rolls.

Note: For spice cake mix, we used Duncan Hines.

LEMON ICE CREAM

This ice cream goes well with the Old-Fashioned Pound Cake on page 126
or the Shortbread Cookie Hearts on page 123.

2 cups sugar
2 cups milk
2 cups half-and-half
2 teaspoons grated lemon rind
1 cup fresh lemon juice
6 drops yellow liquid food coloring
Garnish: fresh mint sprigs

Combine first 6 ingredients. Pour into a 13- x 9-inch pan; freeze at least 2 hours.

Process half of mixture in a food processor until smooth. Remove from processor. Repeat with remaining mixture. Return all of mixture to pan. Freeze 4 hours or until firm. Garnish, if desired. Yield: 1½ quarts.

IRISH CREAM TORTONI CUPS

Reminiscent of a rich Italian tortoni, these frozen dessert cups take on the addition of a smooth liqueur and a cookie base. Pictured on page 46.

¾ cup crushed cream-filled chocolate
    sandwich cookies (10 cookies)
¼ cup boiling water
1 teaspoon instant coffee granules
3 tablespoons grated semisweet chocolate,
    divided
¼ cup Irish cream liqueur
1½ cups whipping cream*
¼ cup sifted powdered sugar*

Line 12 (3-inch) muffin cups with foil muffin liners. Sprinkle 1 tablespoon cookie crumbs in each liner; press lightly.

Combine boiling water and coffee granules, stirring until granules dissolve. Add 1 tablespoon grated chocolate, stirring well. Stir in liqueur, and cool completely.

Beat whipping cream at high speed with an electric mixer until foamy; add sugar, beating until soft peaks form. Gently fold in liqueur mixture. Spoon evenly into muffin liners. Cover; freeze until firm.

Remove from freezer, and let stand 5 minutes before serving. Sprinkle evenly with remaining 2 tablespoons grated chocolate. Yield: 12 servings.

* Substitute 3 cups frozen whipped topping for whipping cream and powdered sugar.

WHITE CHOCOLATE CHARLOTTE RUSSE

For a beautiful presentation, tie a sheer ribbon around this delicate molded dessert.

2 (3.3-ounce) packages white chocolate
    instant pudding mix
2¾ cups milk
2 teaspoons grated orange rind
1 tablespoon Grand Marnier or other
    orange liqueur or orange juice
1 teaspoon vanilla extract
1 cup whipping cream, whipped
19 ladyfingers, split

Prepare pudding mix according to package directions, using 2¾ cups milk. Stir in orange rind, Grand Marnier, and vanilla. Gently fold in whipped cream.

Line bottom and sides of a 9-inch springform pan with ladyfingers. (Simply remove rows of connected ladyfingers intact from their package, unfold them into bottom of pan, and then again around sides of pan.) Spoon pudding mixture into pan. Cover and chill at least 4 hours or until dessert is set.

Place dessert on a serving platter; carefully remove sides of pan. Yield: 12 servings.

Note: We used Jell-O brand pudding mixes.

White Chocolate
Charlotte Russe

CHEESECAKE SAMPLER

This rich, dense New York-style cheesecake received our test kitchens' highest rating—
even without any toppings. Pick from one or all toppings that follow the main recipe.
Pictured on page 140 along with a recipe shortcut idea.

2 cups graham cracker crumbs
½ cup butter or margarine, melted
2 tablespoons sugar
4 (8-ounce) packages cream cheese,
   softened
1¾ cups sugar
7 large eggs
3 (8-ounce) cartons sour cream
1 tablespoon vanilla extract
Cheesecake Toppings

Combine first 3 ingredients; stir well. Press mixture firmly onto bottom and up sides of a lightly greased 9-inch springform pan. Chill thoroughly.

Beat cream cheese at high speed with a heavy-duty electric mixer until fluffy. Gradually add 1¾ cups sugar, beating well. Add eggs, 1 at a time, beating well after each addition. Add sour cream and vanilla; beat at low speed until smooth. Pour into prepared pan. Bake at 300° for 1 hour and 25 min-

utes. Turn off oven, and leave cheesecake in oven 4 hours. (Do not open oven door.)

Remove from oven; cool completely on a wire rack. Cover and chill 8 hours. Remove sides of springform pan; transfer cheesecake to a serving platter. Cut into 8 wedges; top each slice with desired Cheesecake Toppings. Yield: 8 servings.

CHEESECAKE TOPPINGS

ORANGE CHEESECAKE: Brush orange marmalade evenly over slice. Cut candied orange slices in halves, thirds, and quarters. Arrange orange segments over slice.

BLACK-AND-WHITE CHEESECAKE: Spoon one can each ready-made chocolate and cream cheese frostings into separate microwave-safe bowls. Microwave each at HIGH 20 seconds or just until soft and pipeable. Spoon frostings into separate heavy-duty, zip-top plastic bags. Seal; snip a tiny hole in the corner of each bag. Pipe chocolate frosting in a zigzag fashion over slice. Pipe cream cheese frosting over chocolate frosting in the opposite direction. Pipe additional chocolate frosting over cream cheese frosting. Place chocolate-covered coffee beans on crust edge, using chocolate frosting to secure in place.

COCONUT CHEESECAKE: Spoon one can ready-made cream cheese frosting into a microwave-safe bowl. Microwave at HIGH 40 seconds or until melted and pourable. Pour over slice; sprinkle with grated fresh or frozen coconut, thawed.

WALNUT CHEESECAKE: Spoon walnuts-in-syrup ice cream topping over slice. (We used Smucker's.)

PEPPERMINT CHEESECAKE: Spoon one can ready-made cream cheese frosting into a microwave-safe bowl. Microwave at HIGH 30 seconds or until almost melted and stirrable. Combine frosting and crushed peppermint candy; stir well. Spread over slice. Place whole pillow-shaped peppermint candies around crust edge.

RASPBERRY CHEESECAKE: Brush melted seedless raspberry jam over slice. Arrange fresh raspberries over slice; brush lightly with additional melted jam.

CAFÉ AU LAIT CHEESECAKE: Spoon sweetened whipped cream or thawed frozen whipped topping into a decorating bag fitted with a large star tip. Pipe rosettes over slice, and sprinkle evenly with ground cinnamon. Place a pirouline cookie on the crust edge of slice.

HOLLY CHEESECAKE: Pipe green cake decorating gel in shape of holly leaves over slice. Arrange 3 red candy-coated chocolate-covered peanuts at top of leaves.

GERMAN CHOCOLATE PIE

Your guests will rave about the crusty coconut top and the chesslike fudgy filling.

Pastry for 10-inch pie
1 (4-ounce) package sweet baking chocolate
¼ cup butter or margarine
1 (12-ounce) can evaporated milk
1½ cups sugar
3 tablespoons cornstarch
⅛ teaspoon salt
2 large eggs
1 teaspoon vanilla extract
⅔ cup flaked coconut
⅓ cup chopped pecans
1 cup sweetened whipped cream
3 tablespoons chocolate shavings

Place pastry in a 9½-inch deep-dish pieplate. Set aside.

Combine baking chocolate and butter in a medium saucepan; cook over low heat, stirring until chocolate melts. Remove from heat, and gradually stir in evaporated milk; set aside.

Combine sugar, cornstarch, and salt in a large bowl; add eggs and vanilla, mixing well. Gradually stir in chocolate mixture, using a wire whisk. Pour mixture into unbaked pastry shell, and sprinkle with coconut and pecans.

Bake at 375° for 45 minutes. (Pie may appear soft, but will become firm after cooling.) Cool at least 4 hours. Top pie with whipped cream and chocolate shavings. Yield: 1 (9½-inch) pie.

PASTRY FOR 10-INCH PIE

1½ cups all-purpose flour
¾ teaspoon salt
½ cup shortening
4 to 5 tablespoons ice water

Combine flour and salt; cut in shortening with a pastry blender until mixture is crumbly. Sprinkle ice water, 1 tablespoon at a time, evenly over surface; stir with a fork until dry ingredients are moistened. Shape into a ball; cover and chill until ready to use.

Roll pastry to ⅛-inch thickness on a lightly floured surface. Place in pieplate; trim off excess pastry along edges. Fold edges under, and crimp. Chill. Yield: 1 pastry shell.

BROWNIE-MINT PIE

Brownie mix is the secret behind this quick and easy pie.

1 (4.6-ounce) package chocolate mints
1 (15.8-ounce) package brownie mix
1 unbaked (9-inch) deep-dish frozen
    pastry shell
Vanilla ice cream
Hot fudge topping

Chop chocolate mints, and set 3 table-spoons aside. Prepare brownie according to package directions, stirring remaining chopped chocolate mints into batter. Pour mixture into pastry shell.

Bake at 350° for 45 minutes or until center is firm to the touch; cool slightly. Serve with ice cream, hot fudge topping, and reserved 3 tablespoons chopped mints. Yield: 1 (9-inch) pie.

Note: We used Andes chocolate mints.

BRANDIED EGGNOG TRIFLE

Serve this tempting trifle in wine glasses as shown at left or in a trifle bowl as seen on page 46.

1 quart refrigerated eggnog, divided
2 envelopes unflavored gelatin
¼ cup brandy, divided
1 teaspoon vanilla extract
3 cups frozen whipped topping, thawed and divided
1 (16-ounce) frozen pound cake loaf, thawed
5 cups sliced fresh strawberries
1 cup strawberry preserves
Garnish: toasted sliced almonds

Place 1 cup eggnog in a medium saucepan; sprinkle with gelatin. Let stand 1 minute. Cook over low heat, stirring gently, until gelatin completely dissolves. Stir in remaining eggnog, 2 tablespoons brandy, and vanilla. Remove from heat. Chill until consistency of unbeaten egg white (about 15 minutes). Fold in 1 cup whipped topping; chill until softly set. Cut cake into cubes.

To layer dessert in a trifle bowl, arrange enough strawberry slices, cut sides out, to go around lower edge of a 4-quart trifle bowl.

Place half of pound cake cubes in bowl; sprinkle with 1 tablespoon brandy.

Combine remaining strawberries and preserves. Spoon half of strawberry mixture over pound cake; top with half of eggnog mixture. Top with remaining pound cake, and sprinkle with remaining 1 tablespoon brandy. Spoon remaining strawberry mixture over pound cake; then spoon remaining eggnog mixture over strawberries.

Spread remaining 2 cups whipped topping over trifle. Cover and chill at least 1 hour. Garnish, if desired. Yield: 14 servings.

Variation: To serve this trifle in wine glasses, layer ingredients as directed for the trifle bowl, dividing them evenly to fill the wine glasses. Or prepare dessert in trifle bowl as directed, and just spoon trifle into wine glasses.

Note: Two 16-ounce packages of frozen whole strawberries can be substituted for 5 cups fresh strawberries. Just place whole strawberries in bottom of bowl. (If you slice them, they become mushy.)

NO-TIME-TO-COOK DESSERTS

《 》

Whether you're hosting a dessert party or looking for something sweet for the end of a meal, these no-cook treats are sure to satisfy.

THIS TAKES THE CAKE

Cheesecake, that is. The frozen cheesecakes you'll find at food warehouses and super-stores are an easy alternative when you don't have time to make your own. Adorn 《《 them with your choice of toppings (see pages 134–135) to personalize them a bit. Top cream cheese icing with items such as coconut, candies, or jellies and fruit. Or pipe whipped topping in decorative patterns on top.

SUPER SUNDAE

What could be easier than an ice cream
sundae bar? Fill serving bowls with
favorite toppings such as hot fudge,
whipped cream, nuts, cookies, candies,
and fruit—then let the fun begin.

«

^

BEST OF THE BAKERY

Guests will never know a bakery cake isn't
homemade when you transfer it to a pretty cake
stand and embellish it with flowers and ribbon.

DREAM CREAM

Make homemade ice cream sandwiches by placing
« your favorite ice cream between two wafer cookies. Wrap individually in plastic wrap, and freeze
up to 1 month—if they hang around that long.

METRIC EQUIVALENTS

The recipes that appear in this cookbook use the standard United States method for measuring liquid and dry or solid ingredients (teaspoons, tablespoons, and cups). The information on this chart is provided to help cooks outside the U.S. successfully use these recipes. All equivalents are approximate.

EQUIVALENTS FOR DIFFERENT TYPES OF INGREDIENTS

A standard cup measure of a dry or solid ingredient will vary in weight depending on the type of ingredient. A standard cup of liquid is the same volume for any type of liquid. Use the following chart when converting standard cup measures to grams (weight) or milliliters (volume).

Standard Cup	Fine Powder (ex. flour)	Grain (ex. rice)	Granular (ex. sugar)	Liquid Solids (ex. butter)	Liquid (ex. milk)
1	140 g	150 g	190 g	200 g	240 ml
¾	105 g	113 g	143 g	150 g	180 ml
⅔	93 g	100 g	125 g	133 g	160 ml
½	70 g	75 g	95 g	100 g	120 ml
⅓	47 g	50 g	63 g	67 g	80 ml
¼	35 g	38 g	48 g	50 g	60 ml
⅛	18 g	19 g	24 g	25 g	30 ml

EQUIVALENTS FOR LIQUID INGREDIENTS BY VOLUME

¼ tsp					=	1 ml	
½ tsp					=	2 ml	
1 tsp					=	5 ml	
3 tsp	=	1 tbls		=	½ fl oz	=	15 ml	
		2 tbls	=	⅛ cup	=	1 fl oz	=	30 ml	
		4 tbls	=	¼ cup	=	2 fl oz	=	60 ml	
		5⅓ tbls	=	⅓ cup	=	3 fl oz	=	80 ml	
		8 tbls	=	½ cup	=	4 fl oz	=	120 ml	
		10⅔ tbls	=	⅔ cup	=	5 fl oz	=	160 ml	
		12 tbls	=	¾ cup	=	6 fl oz	=	180 ml	
		16 tbls	=	1 cup	=	8 fl oz	=	240 ml	
		1 pt	=	2 cups	=	16 fl oz	=	480 ml	
		1 qt	=	4 cups	=	32 fl oz	=	960 ml	
						33 fl oz	=	1000 ml	= 1 liter

EQUIVALENTS FOR DRY INGREDIENTS BY WEIGHT

(To convert ounces to grams, multiply the number of ounces by 30.)

1 oz	=	¹⁄₁₆ lb	=	30 g
4 oz	=	¼ lb	=	120 g
8 oz	=	½ lb	=	240 g
12 oz	=	¾ lb	=	360 g
16 oz	=	1 lb	=	480 g

EQUIVALENTS FOR LENGTH

(To convert inches to centimeters, multiply the number of inches by 2.5.)

1 in			=	2.5 cm	
6 in	=	½ ft	=	15 cm	
12 in	=	1 ft	=	30 cm	
36 in	=	3 ft = 1 yd	=	90 cm	
40 in			=	100 cm	= 1 meter

EQUIVALENTS FOR COOKING/OVEN TEMPERATURES

	Fahrenheit	Celsius	Gas Mark
Freeze Water	32° F	0° C	
Room Temperature	68° F	20° C	
Boil Water	212° F	100° C	
Bake	325° F	160° C	3
	350° F	180° C	4
	375° F	190° C	5
	400° F	200° C	6
	425° F	220° C	7
	450° F	230° C	8
Broil			Grill

SUPER SUNDAE

What could be easier than an ice cream
sundae bar? Fill serving bowls with
favorite toppings such as hot fudge,
whipped cream, nuts, cookies, candies,
and fruit—then let the fun begin.

BEST OF THE BAKERY

Guests will never know a bakery cake isn't
homemade when you transfer it to a pretty cake
stand and embellish it with flowers and ribbon.

DREAM CREAM

Make homemade ice cream sandwiches by placing
your favorite ice cream between two wafer cookies. Wrap individually in plastic wrap, and freeze
up to 1 month—if they hang around that long.

METRIC EQUIVALENTS

The recipes that appear in this cookbook use the standard United States method for measuring liquid and dry or solid ingredients (teaspoons, tablespoons, and cups). The information on this chart is provided to help cooks outside the U.S. successfully use these recipes. All equivalents are approximate.

EQUIVALENTS FOR DIFFERENT TYPES OF INGREDIENTS

A standard cup measure of a dry or solid ingredient will vary in weight depending on the type of ingredient. A standard cup of liquid is the same volume for any type of liquid. Use the following chart when converting standard cup measures to grams (weight) or milliliters (volume).

Standard Cup	Fine Powder	Grain	Granular	Liquid Solids	Liquid
	(ex. flour)	(ex. rice)	(ex. sugar)	(ex. butter)	(ex. milk)
1	140 g	150 g	190 g	200 g	240 ml
¾	105 g	113 g	143 g	150 g	180 ml
⅔	93 g	100 g	125 g	133 g	160 ml
½	70 g	75 g	95 g	100 g	120 ml
⅓	47 g	50 g	63 g	67 g	80 ml
¼	35 g	38 g	48 g	50 g	60 ml
⅛	18 g	19 g	24 g	25 g	30 ml

EQUIVALENTS FOR LIQUID INGREDIENTS BY VOLUME

¼ tsp				=	1 ml	
½ tsp				=	2 ml	
1 tsp				=	5 ml	
3 tsp	=	1 tbls		= ½ fl oz =	15 ml	
		2 tbls	= ⅛ cup	= 1 fl oz =	30 ml	
		4 tbls	= ¼ cup	= 2 fl oz =	60 ml	
		5⅓ tbls	= ⅓ cup	= 3 fl oz =	80 ml	
		8 tbls	= ½ cup	= 4 fl oz =	120 ml	
		10⅔ tbls	= ⅔ cup	= 5 fl oz =	160 ml	
		12 tbls	= ¾ cup	= 6 fl oz =	180 ml	
		16 tbls	= 1 cup	= 8 fl oz =	240 ml	
		1 pt	= 2 cups	= 16 fl oz =	480 ml	
		1 qt	= 4 cups	= 32 fl oz =	960 ml	
				33 fl oz =	1000 ml	= 1 liter

EQUIVALENTS FOR DRY INGREDIENTS BY WEIGHT

(To convert ounces to grams, multiply the number of ounces by 30.)

1 oz	=	¹⁄₁₆ lb	=	30 g
4 oz	=	¼ lb	=	120 g
8 oz	=	½ lb	=	240 g
12 oz	=	¾ lb	=	360 g
16 oz	=	1 lb	=	480 g

EQUIVALENTS FOR LENGTH

(To convert inches to centimeters, multiply the number of inches by 2.5.)

1 in			= 2.5 cm	
6 in	= ½ ft		= 15 cm	
12 in	= 1 ft		= 30 cm	
36 in	= 3 ft	= 1 yd	= 90 cm	
40 in			= 100 cm	= 1 meter

EQUIVALENTS FOR COOKING/OVEN TEMPERATURES

	Fahrenheit	Celsius	Gas Mark
Freeze Water	32° F	0° C	
Room Temperature	68° F	20° C	
Boil Water	212° F	100° C	
Bake	325° F	160° C	3
	350° F	180° C	4
	375° F	190° C	5
	400° F	200° C	6
	425° F	220° C	7
	450° F	230° C	8
Broil			Grill

RECIPE INDEX

NO-COOK RECIPE IDEAS